The World
in the
Postwar Decade

1945 – 1955

BOOKS BY J. HAMPDEN JACKSON

A HISTORY OF ENGLAND
(*with C. E. Carrington*)

EUROPE SINCE THE WAR

THE BETWEEN-WAR WORLD

ENGLAND SINCE THE INDUSTRIAL REVOLUTION

FINLAND

ESTONIA

JAURÈS, HIS LIFE AND WORK

CLEMENCEAU AND THE THIRD REPUBLIC

THE WORLD IN THE
POSTWAR DECADE, 1945–1955

The World
in the . N 106
Postwar Decade

1945–1955

BY

J. HAMPDEN JACKSON

HOUGHTON MIFFLIN COMPANY BOSTON

𝕿𝖍𝖊 𝕽𝖎𝖛𝖊𝖗𝖘𝖎𝖉𝖊 𝕻𝖗𝖊𝖘𝖘 𝕮𝖆𝖒𝖇𝖗𝖎𝖉𝖌𝖊

1956

The Riverside Press
CAMBRIDGE • MASSACHUSETTS
PRINTED IN THE U.S.A.

INTRODUCTION

IN THE DECADE 1945–55 the world was preoccupied with two issues. The first was rivalry between the Soviet Union and the United States, a rivalry which began in nominal partnership but soon turned into an armaments race and a cold war, dividing all Europe and part of Asia into armed camps, aligning every industrial Power in the world on one side or the other and threatening to break out into fighting which would mean a third world war. The second was the nationalist movement for independence in countries which were dominated politically or financially by the white man. The peoples of Latin America, the Middle East, Africa and most of southern Asia were not interested in the struggle between the Great Powers; they were preoccupied with gaining their own independence.

The two issues rarely overlapped. Only when a movement for national independence seemed to be thwarted by an imperialist Power did its leaders seek support from Communist Russia and thus take sides in the Great Power conflict; this was the case in China and to some extent in Indochina, but nowhere else. The issues remained separate, and the history of the world in this postwar decade therefore has two themes, which are treated severally in the first two parts of this book. The third part describes internal developments in the Soviet Union, the United Kingdom and the United States — developments on which much of the outside world depended.

CONTENTS

Contents

Part 3. The Great Powers at Home

MAPS

Part One

THE GREAT-POWER CONFLICT

CHAPTER 1

THE JOINT SETTLEMENT

THE POSTWAR AGE may be counted as beginning in February 1945 when Churchill, Roosevelt and Stalin met in conference at Yalta in the Crimea. The war was not yet over on any front: the Germans were holding the frontiers of the Reich everywhere except in East Prussia and Silesia, which had been overrun by the Russians, and they still held Budapest and northern Italy; the Japanese were still undefeated in their home islands. But the end was in sight. It was confidently reckoned that two or three more months' fighting would see the capitulation of Germany and that the Japanese war would be brought to an end within eighteen months after that.

The time had come to take decisions about the postwar world. The leaders of the three Great Powers had met before to discuss these problems. At Teheran in November 1943, for instance, they had reached agreement about general aims. An allied conference had been meeting in the United States in 1944 to work out the constitution of a world organization, later to be known as the United Nations. Agreements had been reached in London in the autumn of 1944 about the zones of military occupation for which Britain, the United States and the Soviet Union would be responsible when the allied forces entered Germany. But now that the rapid end of the war was no longer in doubt, agreements of a more specific and far-reaching nature had to be reached. It was for that purpose that Churchill and Roosevelt met at Malta and set out on the long, cold flight to the Crimea.

It was already obvious to everyone that power politics in the future would be a matter for the United States and the Soviet Union. In Europe there could be no continental state or combination of continental states which would be able to counterbalance the Russians. Germany was on the verge of unconditional surrender. The damage done to France, moral and physical, was such that she could not be counted on to play her old role as a Great Power at any time in the foreseeable future. There would be a vacuum in Europe which must be filled either by the three Great Powers jointly or else by the Soviet Union and by the United States (together with Britain) in competition. Alone, Britain could take no great part in continental affairs: she was immediately dependent on loans from the United States, and it was clear that her economic dependence must continue for some time.

It was the same in the Far East. Japan was about to be defeated and China was in a state of chaos, but the old imperial position of Britain in the eastern Pacific could not be restored. The future lay with the United States, which was mounting the final assault upon Japan and was the patron on which the Kuomintang government of China depended, and with the Soviet Union, which was a Far Eastern Power in its own right. No other Power could be expected to have any major influence in eastern Asia within the next decade. The only question, there as in Europe, was whether the United States and the Soviet Union would act in concert or in opposition.

To public opinion in 1944 there was no doubt as to what the answer must be. All over the English-speaking world there was admiration verging on adulation for the Soviet peoples and for their leaders. One could scarcely say "Red Army" in those days without putting the adjective "glorious" before it; one could not talk of Russians without praising their endurance, self-sacrifice and heroism. Stalin was "Uncle Joe" to the English-speaking masses, as he was to Churchill and Roosevelt in their private correspondence. No democratic leader would have dared to say a public word against the intentions of the Kremlin even if he had wanted to. There was no alternative to working with Stalin and his colleagues. Victory would not have been in prospect without the alliance of the three Great Powers; without their continued alliance, a peace settlement was unthinkable. There must be a joint settlement or none.

It was realized, of course, by Churchill and Roosevelt that joint settlement would be easier said than made. At the height of the fighting, when collaboration between the three Great Powers had been most vitally necessary, Western leaders had found Russia "a surly and suspicious ally." Once the bond of war against the German enemy was removed, there would be difficulties. But most disagreements in the past had been removed by a personal interview with Stalin, and now when the last battles against the common enemies were still being fought was the time to settle postwar problems round the table with Uncle Joe. It was in this mood that Churchill and Roosevelt set out for the Crimea.

THE YALTA CONFERENCE

Among the myriad questions discussed at various levels at Yalta, three were of the greatest importance. The first concerned the composition of the world organization (the name

United Nations had not yet been decided) on which so much of the future harmony of the world seemed to depend. On this the Soviet leaders were cooperative and conciliatory. Stalin withdrew his request for sixteen votes in the Assembly and declared that he would be content with three — that is, with seats for Belorussia and Ukraine as well as for the Soviet Union. When the question arose of the Great Powers' rights in the Security Council, it was Roosevelt, not Stalin, who insisted on their right of veto. The Americans were anxious that no decision should be taken against the will of the United States on any major matter. Roosevelt therefore suggested that every important decision should require the concurring votes of the Big Four, namely the United States, the Soviet Union, Britain and China. It was a suggestion with which Stalin and Churchill were pleased to agree.

The German question raised no great difficulties. Stalin withdrew his objection to France's having a share of the British and American zones and a seat on the Control Commission. He pressed for a large sum to be paid to Russia in reparations, and when Churchill opposed this it was agreed that a special commission should be set up in Moscow to work out reparations proposals in secret.

It was the Polish question that gave the most trouble at Yalta, where it was discussed at seven of the eight plenary meetings of the Conference. The points at issue were how to form a provisional government for Poland and where to draw the Polish frontiers. On both of these Stalin had very decided views. The provisional government should be the Soviet-sponsored Lublin Committee, which would have nothing to do with the so-called Polish government in London, especially now that that body had dismissed the leader of the Polish Peasant Party, Mikolajczyk, for being ready to negotiate with the Lubliners. Churchill and Roosevelt were strongly of the opinion that the Lublin Committee, which the Russians persisted in calling the Warsaw government, should be supplemented by acknowledged leaders of Polish political opinion both from London and from inside Poland. In the end a formula was found for agreement: the Lublin Committee would be reorganized by the inclusion of democratic leaders from at home and abroad, and this provisional government would make itself responsible for holding free elections at the first possible opportunity.

On the matter of frontiers there was no disagreement in principle. Churchill and Roosevelt were ready to recognize that Poland east of the Curzon Line should be handed over to Russia, and that Poland should be compensated by being given German territory in East Prussia (not including Königsberg and its hinterland, which was to go to Russia) and in the west. The only question was how far to the west. Stalin suggested as far as Stettin and then along the line of the Oder and the western Neisse. This last point was too much for Roosevelt, who told Stalin that he agreed that Poland should receive compensation from Germany "including that portion of East Prussia south of the Königsberg line, Upper Silesia, and up to the line of the Oder," but added that "there would appear to be little justification for extending it up to the western Neisse." The conclusion was that the final delimitation of the western frontier of Poland should be left until the Peace Conference.

Neither the American nor the British representatives at Yalta were comfortable about the decisions reached on the Polish question. Edward R. Stettinius, who was present as United States Secretary of State, noted in his book *Roosevelt and the Russians: The Yalta Conference* that "by February 1945 Poland and all eastern Europe except for most of Czechoslovakia was in the hands of the Red Army. *As a result of this situation it was not a question of what Great Britain and the United States would permit Russia to do in Poland, but of what the two countries could persuade the Soviet Union to accept.*" Churchill, who had twenty-five M.P.'s voting against him in the House of Commons after the Yalta debate and twenty-five of his own members abstaining, wrote in *The Second World War*: "It is easy, after the Germans are beaten, to condemn those who did their best to hearten the Russian military effort and to keep in harmonious contact with our great Ally, who had suffered so frightfully. What would have happened if we had quarrelled with Russia while the Germans still had two or three hundred divisions on the fighting front? Our hopeful assumptions were soon to be falsified. Still, they were the only possible ones at the time."

The determination to base the postwar world on a joint settlement between the three Great Powers was shown most clearly by the secret agreement made at Yalta to extend Russian influence in the Far East. The Americans were naturally anxious to have Russian help in the forthcoming campaigns against Japan, and both they and the British at Yalta were willing to pay Stalin his price. He demanded, in return for his undertaking that the Soviet Union would declare war on Japan within two or three months after the German surrender, that Russia should be given southern Sakhalin and the Kurile Islands, Russian control of Outer Mongolia should be recognized and Russia should be restored to the position in Manchuria which she had held in 1904. These last two demands would involve concessions by China; both Outer Mongolia and Manchuria had been part of the Chinese Empire. Russia's claims of Manchuria involved joint Chinese-Soviet control of the railways, the recognition of the pre-eminent interests of Russia in the commercial port of Dairen and the lease of Port Arthur as a Soviet naval base. Roosevelt undertook to bring

Miles

0   50   100   150

NETHERLANDS

BELGIUM

LUXEMBOURG

SAAR

FRANCE

GERMAN

FEDERAL

REPUBLIC

SWITZERLAND

GERMAN

Szczecin
(Stettin)

Berlin

DEMOCRATIC

REPUBLIC

POLAND

Oder

Neisse

CZECHOSLOVAKIA

AUSTRIA

ITALY

Trieste

Russian Zone		British Zone
American "		French "

pressure on Chiang Kai-shek to induce him to make these concessions. There could have been no doubt in anyone's mind that the Soviet Union would thereby be established as a military, naval and air power in the northeastern Pacific.

When the Yalta Conference ended it was understood that the war against both Germany and Japan would be fought to an end by the three Great Powers in close alliance and that the same close alliance would be the basis of the peace settlements. There were some doubts in British minds as to Stalin's good intentions, but Churchill did his best to allay them by a speech in the House of Commons on February 27: "The impression I brought back from the Crimea, and from all my other contacts, is that Marshal Stalin and the other Soviet leaders wish to live in honourable partnership and equality with the Western democracies. I feel also that their word is their bond. I know of no Government which stands to its obligations, even in its own despite, more solidly than the Russian Government. I decline absolutely to embark here on a discussion about Russian good faith."

There was a good deal more doubt in Russian minds about Churchill's good intentions. He was known to be in favor of a Western offensive in Istria and Slovenia which would keep Russian influence away from the Adriatic and perhaps from Austria as well, and he was rightly suspected of wanting British and American troops to advance as far as possible into Germany and thereafter to refuse to retire behind the frontier of their zone of occupation as agreed in the autumn of 1944. The United States government, first under Roosevelt and after his death in April 1945 under Truman, did its best to remove these Russian doubts. Thanks to its insistence, the liberation of Vienna, Prague and Berlin from the Nazis was left to the Red Army, and the Western Allies withdrew westward to their agreed zones of occupation in Germany and Austria in July 1945.

THE POTSDAM CONFERENCE

In spite of the United States' good offices, the atmosphere was uneasy when the Big Three met for their first postwar conference at Potsdam in July. Hitler was dead, Germany had surrendered unconditionally, the most complete victory in European history had been won. But its very completeness involved appalling danger and responsibilities. There was the responsibility of rebuilding the greater part of Europe, especially Germany, which was in a state of unparalleled ruin, physical, moral and political. There was the danger, now that the primary purpose of the great alliance had been removed by victory, of the allies each going its own way, of Americans removing their troops and their influence from Europe and of the Russians taking the fruits of victory for their own consumption. The urgent need at the Potsdam Conference was to make decisions that would bind the Big Three together.

The first problem at Potsdam was to reach agreement in the treatment of Germany. It was easy to agree on demilitarization and denazification, easy to say that "German education shall be so controlled as completely to eliminate Nazi and militarist doctrines and to make possible the successful development of democratic ideas." It was not difficult to decide that no German government should be recognized, for there was no immediate possibility of finding one in the vacuum left after twelve years of Nazi tyranny. There must be a period of joint allied control during which German democracy would be built up from the bottom. In the Potsdam Agreement, signed by Stalin, Truman and Attlee (who had succeeded Churchill as Prime Minister of the United Kingdom while the Conference was sitting), it was laid down that

The administration of affairs in Germany should be directed towards the decentralization of the political structure and the development of local responsibility. To this end (i) local self-government shall be restored throughout Germany on democratic principles . . .; (ii) all democratic political parties with rights of assembly and of public discussion shall be allowed and encouraged throughout Germany; (iii) representative and elective principles shall be introduced into regional, provincial and State [land] administration as rapidly as may be justified by the successful applications of these principles in local self-government; (iv) for the time being no central German Government shall be established. Nothwithstanding this, however, certain essential central German administrative departments, headed by State Secretaries, shall be established, particularly in the fields of finance, transport, communications, foreign trade, and industry. Such departments will act under the direction of the Control Council.

It is worth noting these last two sentences. Germany was divided into zones of military occupation, but there was no division of Germany for other purposes. Central German administrative departments were to be responsible for the finance, transport, etc., of the whole of Germany, and they were to be under the direction, not of each occupying power in its respective zone, but of the Control Council, comprising Russian, British, American and French representatives. The same point was stressed in the economic clauses of the Potsdam Agreement:

During the period of occupation Germany shall be treated as a single economic unit. To this end common policies shall be established in regard to: (a) mining and industrial production and allocation; (b) agriculture, forestry and fishing; (c) wages, prices and rationing; (d) import and export programs for Germany as a whole; (e) currency and banking, central taxation, and customs; (f) reparation and removal of industrial war potential; (g) transportation and communications.

It was emphasized that the Control Council should determine "the equitable distribution of essential commodities between the several zones, so as to produce a balanced economy throughout Germany and to reduce the needs for imports."

The obvious danger that each occupying power would take reparations from its own zone in such a way as to disrupt that balance was met by the undertaking that "Payments of reparations should leave enough resources to enable the German people to subsist without external assistance." Subject to this consideration, it was agreed that the Soviet Union's reparation claims would be met by removal from the Soviet zone and those of the Western Powers from their zones. The difficulty here was that the capital equipment most needed by the Russians lay in the Ruhr, which was in the British zone. Russia was therefore entitled to

> receive additionally from the Western zones: (a) 15 per cent of such usable and complete capital equipment . . . as is unnecessary for the German peace economy and should be removed from the Western zones of Germany, in exchange for an equivalent value of food, coal, potash, zinc, timber, clay-products, petroleum products or such other commodities as may be agreed upon; (b) 10 per cent of such industrial capital equipment . . . without payment or exchange of any kind in return.

Thus, on the German question the three Great Powers were agreed: they would treat Germany as a single economic unit, in spite of the division into zones of military occupation, and they would work at building a democracy in Germany. Whether they were agreed on the meaning of democracy remained to be seen. In any case, the Potsdam Conference was not the place or the time for attempting a definition.

When it came to the Polish question, the doubts and controversies which had arisen at Yalta arose again in more acute form. In the meantime the Western Powers had withdrawn recognition from the Polish government in London and had recognized as the provisional government of Poland the old Lublin Committee, reorganized by the addition of Miko-lajczyk and one or two other non-Communist leaders. But this government had shown no sign of making preparations for a general election. In the Potsdam Agreement, to which the first signature was Stalin's, it was stated that

> the three Powers note that the Polish Provisional Government, in accordance with the decisions of the Crimea [Yalta] Con-ference, have agreed to the holding of free and unfettered elec-tions as soon as possible on the basis of universal suffrage and secret ballot, in which all democratic and anti-Nazi parties shall have the right to take part and to put forward candidates, and that the representatives of the allied press shall enjoy full free-dom to report to the world upon developments in Poland before and during elections.

On the matter of Poland's western frontiers, Stalin could not be moved from the position he had taken at Yalta. The Western Powers refused to recognize as permanent the fron-tiers which the Poles in fact held, and in the Potsdam Agree-ment "the three heads of Government reaffirm their opinion that the final delimitation of the western frontier of Poland should await the peace settlement." But it had to be agreed that, pending the settlement, the western territories which Stalin had demanded for Poland should be "under the ad-ministration of the Polish State."

The Polish annexation of German territory had meant the expulsion of millions of Germans, who were now refugees in the occupied zones, mostly in the west. Hungary was also expelling her German citizens, and Czechoslovakia was de-termined to expel the Sudeten Deutsch and all other citizens of German extraction, whether they had favored the Nazis or had been persecuted by them. This involved not only human misery and injustice on an unprecedented scale, but serious problems in the occupied zones of Germany, where incalculable numbers of refugees had to be fed, housed and settled. At Potsdam the Western leaders tried to get Stalin to use his influence to check the flood. All they could obtain was a declaration that "any transfers to Germany of German populations should be effected in an orderly and humane manner," and that the Control Council should "submit an estimate of the time and rate at which further transfers could be carried out, having regard to the present situation in Germany."

THE ATOMIC BOMB

There remained the question of Japan. When the Potsdam Conference met the United States fleet was concentrating its attack on her islands and Russian armies were moving eastward in preparation for the day when the Soviet Union would declare war. On July 17 news reached Truman at Potsdam, and was immediately communicated to Churchill, that an experimental explosion in the Mexican desert of the first atomic bomb had been a success. There was no doubt now in American minds that the new weapon could force Japan to surrender — and, as Churchill has recorded, Britain's "consent in principle to the use of this bomb had been given on July 4, before the test had taken place." Truman and Churchill agreed that "we should not need the Russians." Not till July 24, when Truman spoke to Stalin after the adjournment of a concluding session of the Conference, were the Russians told that the Americans had a new weapon. Stalin seemed hardly interested; he asked no questions. Churchill writes: "I was certain therefore that at that date Stalin had no special knowledge of the vast process of research upon which the United States and Britain had been engaged for so long, and of the production for which the United States had spent over four hundred million pounds in an heroic gamble."

If only for their secrecy over the atomic bomb, Stalin had reason to distrust his Western Allies. If only for his conduct in Poland, the Western Powers had reason to distrust Stalin. The remarkable thing is that in spite of all distrust an agreement was reached at Potsdam which put the three Great Powers under an obligation to work together in Germany. On their readiness to fulfill this obligation the prospects of joint settlement, on which alone world peace could be founded, would depend. The machinery had been set up: for Germany, the Control Council; for the preparation of the general peace settlement, the Council of Foreign Ministers of the first principal powers (France and China as well as the Soviet Union, the United Kingdom and the United States); for still wider cooperation concerning the world's welfare, the United Nations Organization. All that was needed now was the good will.

CHAPTER 2

AGREEMENT BREAKS DOWN

THE WAR AGAINST Japan ended a few weeks after the Potsdam Conference broke up. On August 6, 1945, the Americans dropped the first atomic bomb on Hiroshima. On August 8 the Soviet Union declared war against Japan. On August 14 the Japanese surrendered. The three Great Powers were now masters of the world. Never before in history had an alliance held such a global preponderance.

They were not happy in their victory, it involved too many problems. The Americans had suddenly to realize that the United States was the greatest power in the world. It had in fact held that position for some time, but the realization was new. The position was unlike that enjoyed or suffered by any of the world's greatest powers in the past: the United States' superiority to any possible rival was greater than that of any previous "top nation." In the atomic bomb, of which the Americans alone held the secrets, they had a weapon against which no one yet knew any means of defense. In industrial productive capacity they were so far ahead of the Soviet Union and the United Kingdom as to make these powers poor relations rather than equal allies. If the world were to be made free, in the words of Roosevelt's promise, "from fear and from want," there could be no going back to the normalcy and isolation which American administrations had aimed at after the First World War. Fear must be allayed by the sacrifice of the atomic bomb monopoly. Want must be relieved by the spending — by the giving away — of American money on a huge scale. This would not merely be alms-giving; it would be obvious common sense, for American prosperity depended on overseas markets and the pump of those markets must be primed with dollars. But common sense is more easily felt than acted on; it would need a great effort on the part of American administrations to convince their people of the responsibilities of being the world's greatest power.

The difficulties of Great Britain were of an opposite nature. The British people had to realize what they should have realized long before, that their nation was no longer what it had been in the nineteenth century. Britannia could no longer rule the waves: that was now a matter of air power which she could not afford, of access to oil fuel of which she could not be sure. Victory in two world wars had been won only with the support of the United States. Britain could no longer hope to defend herself against a continental enemy without American help, and that would mean the humiliation of asking the United States to maintain a strategic air force on stations in England. Economically the inferiority of Britain was even more obvious. She was no longer the world's fuel supplier — she could hardly raise enough coal for her own needs, let alone for export; no longer the world's banker — that position had passed from London to New York; she could no longer pay for her necessary imports of food and raw material by drawing on her investments abroad — those had vanished in the effort to pay for the war. Immediately Britain was dependent on the good offices of the United States. In the long run she would almost certainly be depend-

ent on American military assistance. The realization of this
would mean a great psychological difficulty for the British
people. For the British government it would involve the most
delicate conduct of relations with Washington and Moscow.

For the Russians the outcome of the war involved a strange
mixture of grandeur and misery. They had won, and they
could feel, remembering the battle of Stalingrad and the great
victories that had followed, that it was largely due to their
own efforts and sacrifices that Nazi Germany had been defeated. They had added twenty-four million European people
to their Union by annexing Estonia, Latvia, Lithuania, East
Poland, Bessarabia and northern Bukovina, Ruthenia, parts
of Finland and part of East Prussia. They had established
their control over another eighty-seven million people by the
Red Army's occupation of Europe as far west as a line from
Lübeck to Trieste. But they had suffered vastly more in loss
of lives, property and productive capacity than either of the
other great victors, and they felt nothing but apprehension at
the knowledge that the atomic bomb was in the hands of the
Americans.

Two things the Russians lacked which the Americans and
the British could feel themselves to possess in comparative
sufficiency. The first was security. Russia had been invaded
again and again from the west — by Napoleon, by Wilhelm
II, by Poland and a host of Western Powers after 1917, by
Hitler in 1941. How could her western frontier be made
secure in the future? The choice was between alliance with
the United States and Great Britain — two capitalist powers
which on the Marxist hypothesis could not be trusted — and
an attempt to use the position as occupying power in Eastern
and Central Europe to erect a deep buffer between Russia
and the West.

The other great need of Russia was machinery. How backward she was in industrial production, how lacking in capital

equipment and in skilled technicians the outside world hardly realized. The Soviet government had succeeded in turning out first-rate military airplanes and tanks for use during the war, but behind this crust of armor the shortage of machinery was such that the Red Army had had to depend largely on peasant wagons for transport. Russia had abundant resources for industrial production, but before they could be used to raise the standard of living of the people there must be machinery from abroad. The misfortune was that in all areas that had come under Russian control as the result of victory — in all the 191,000 square miles that had been annexed in Europe and in the 392,000 square miles (excluding Yugoslavia) which had been occupied by the Red Army — there was no major industrial area. Some engineering products could be turned out in western Czechoslovakia, Poland, East Germany and Austria, but none of the great founts of industry was in Russian hands. The Ruhr, in particular, was in the British zone of Germany. The British had no use for it but were unwilling to let more than a trickle of its products come Russia's way.

These two great needs lay behind Soviet foreign policy in the immediate postwar years. They were not sufficiently appreciated in the West, where the general public, still enthusiastic about the triumphs of the Red Army and sympathetic to the sufferings of the Soviet peoples during the war, could feel nothing but amazement at the successive revelations of what appeared to be a policy of selfish noncooperation and aggrandizement.

RUSSIAN CONDUCT IN GERMANY

On five fronts in the years 1945, 1946 and 1947 the policy of Stalin outraged the Western Powers, to whom it seemed a breach of the agreements he had made at Yalta and at Potsdam. The first, which the Westerners from their position in their respective sectors of Berlin could observe most closely, was Germany. From the outset the Russians treated their zone of occupation as if it were under their unconditional sovereignty. While their representative on the Allied Control Commission kept up a running fire of criticism against his colleagues for alleged breach of the Potsdam Agreement, the Soviet government proceeded as if the Agreement did not exist. Instead of treating Germany as "a single economic unit," they regarded their zonal boundary as if it were an international frontier. Instead of acting "so as to produce a balanced economy throughout Germany and reduce the need for imports," they acted as if East Germany were their prey, removing industrial equipment and crops and setting the Germans to work for Russia. The rest of Germany depended on foodstuffs raised in the eastern zone; since these were no longer available, it had to depend on imports — on gifts from the Western Powers — or else starve. Instead of seeing that "all democratic political parties with rights of assembly and public discussions be allowed and encouraged," public discussion in speech, press and radio was censored or forbidden, rights of assembly were refused, and the only political party that was in any way encouraged was the Communist-dominated Socialist Unity Party formed by the forced fusion of the Socialists with the Communists in the spring of 1946.

RUSSIAN CONDUCT IN POLAND

The second front on which Soviet policy gave a shock to the Western Powers was Poland. Churchill recounts that when Roosevelt asked Stalin at Yalta how soon it would be possible to hold elections in Poland, Stalin replied: "Within a month unless there is some catastrophe on the front, which is impossible." That was in February 1945. The elections were not held till January 1947. Meanwhile Stalin and Molotov had blocked all attempts by the Western leaders to send observers into Poland and to get non-Communist Poles into effective positions in the government. Some leaders of the Polish Underground were invited to Moscow and given a safe-conduct by the Russian political police; they were liquidated. When Mikolajczyk was at last invited to Warsaw, the Lublin Committee had clearly consolidated its power. The 1947 elections were held under a degree of Communist control which made nonsense of any claim that they were "free and unfettered." Mikolajczyk was impotent; in October 1947 he left Poland.

FIVE PEACE TREATIES

A third shock to the Western Powers came over the drawing up of treaties to be imposed on the five European States which had fought on the German side — Hungary, Rumania, Bulgaria, Finland and Italy. This was the first task assigned at Potsdam to the Council of Foreign Ministers. It should have been a simple business, but in fact it led to the most acrimonious and protracted negotiation. In the end Molotov's demands were accepted in the terms for Hungary, Rumania, Bulgaria and Finland — countries which, to put it mildly, were in the Russian sphere of influence — and a great many of his demands were incorporated in the treaty with Italy (see page 63), in whose case the Russians might have been expected to bow to British and American views.

In the treaties with Hungary, Rumania and Bulgaria only one clause is noteworthy. It appears in each treaty in identical words: "Hungary [or Rumania or Bulgaria] shall take all measures necessary to secure to all persons under Hungarian [or Rumanian or Bulgarian] jurisdiction, without distinction as to race, sex, language or religion, the enjoyment of human rights and of fundamental freedoms, including freedom of expression, of press and publication, of religious worship, of political opinion and of public meeting." Since the Soviet Union would be primarily responsible for the observance of the treaties in these countries, it is difficult to see how Molotov can in good faith have allowed this clause to be inserted.

The treaty with Finland followed the lines of the armistice agreement which the Soviet Union had enforced in September 1944. It is interesting in two respects. Contrary to their policy with regard to every other neighbor state in Eastern Europe, the Russians made no military occupation of Finland and attempted little interference with her internal affairs. Yet Finland had fought against the Russians not once but twice during the Second World War: in 1939, when she had refused the Kremlin's demands for Finnish territory, and again in 1941, when she had joined in Germany's attack on the Soviet Union. In the settlement with Finland, the Kremlin thought it sufficient for Russian security that Finland should be deprived of her Karelian province and of her outlet to the Arctic Ocean at Petsamo and that Russia should have a lease of the Porkkala Peninsula for use as a military base. It was in respect of reparations that Finland could be useful to Russia, especially of reparations in the form of machinery and engineering products. Finland was far from being an industrial country. Virtually the only goods she was in the way of exporting were timber and wood products. But Russia demanded goods to the value of 300 million dollars at prices obtaining in 1938, and two-thirds of this value were to be made up of ships and cables and machines of all types, including such highly specialized products as electric motors, for which the Finns had no raw materials, machine tools or the skilled tradesmen. The Russians knew that the Finns, if they were left free, would find a way of making these industrial products and of delivering them on the date specified; therefore the Russians left them free. Russia's crying need for machinery has no better illustration than the terms of the 1944 armistice with Finland and those of the 1947 treaty which confirmed them.

The treaty with Italy should have been largely for Britain and the United States to decide. They had done all the fighting against the Germans in the peninsula and had conducted all the negotiations with the Italian leaders after the fall of Mussolini. They had recognized the Italians as "co-belligerents" after 1943, and had undertaken to treat them kindly in the peace settlement if they "worked their passage" by fighting against the Germans. This the Italians were officially recognized to have done. But on Molotov's insistence the treaty presented to Italy, instead of being one suitable for a co-belligerent that had worked its passage, was a treaty with an ex-enemy deserving punishment.

The drafting of the treaties with the five minor ex-enemy powers had revealed an unfriendly obduracy on the part of the Russians. The Western Powers realized that they must make sacrifices to overcome Russian distrust. They showed extraordinary patience — Ernest Bevin, the British Foreign Secretary, attended no fewer than ninety-five meetings on the question of these minor treaties alone. They made more than reasonable concessions. Russia's attitude augured ill for the policy of joint peace settlement.

Russia's attitude over Austria was even more puzzling. Austria counted not as an ex-enemy but as a liberated nation, and there should have been no difficulty in negotiating peace, for when the Russians entered the country in April 1945 they set up a provisional Austrian government under the veteran Socialist, Dr. Karl Renner, a government which was subsequently recognized by the Western Powers and which obviously had the support of the Austrian people. The United States, Britain and France were in favor of generous terms for Austria while the Russians insisted on having the lion's share of Austrian oil, commerce and industry, but that did not explain the inability to agree on treaty terms, for even when the Western Powers and the Austrian government yielded to Russian demands, the Russians still refused to sign. There was to be no treaty with Austria for many years. A decade after the liberation the little republic was still occupied by the forces of the four Great Powers — "four elephants in a canoe," as Dr. Renner said.

Austria's postwar history was full of surprises. The Russians allowed the Austrian government to organize in the autumn of 1945 a free general election, so free that only four Communist members were returned. They let the republic be governed more or less as a single unit, they took their place with the Western Powers' representatives in the Allied Council in Vienna and made no attempt to sovietize their own zone of occupation. It seemed enough for them to draw the oil from Zistersdorf, to mulct Austria through the Soviet Administration of German Assets in Austria (U.S.I.A.), and to cover the open southern frontier of Czechoslovakia with their troops (see page 35).

The conduct of the Austrians was equally surprising. They refused all blandishments to turn toward Communism — 5 per cent of the votes were the most that Communists could win in any election; they supported solidly and in roughly equal numbers their two great political parties, the Socialists and the Catholics; and those traditionally antagonistic parties combined steadily and fruitfully in coalition governments.

The revival of Austria was one of the most heartening symptoms in the stricken body of central Europe in the postwar years.

THE UNITED NATIONS

A fourth front on which diplomatic battle was waged between the Soviet Union and the Western Powers was the United Nations. The faith in which that organization had been founded was gradually shattered as it became obvious that in the Assembly there was an uncompromising minority of five votes — the three Soviet members, Poland and Yugoslavia — and that in the Security Council there could be no decision on the most important matters because of the refusal of the Soviet representative to concur. It had been the intention of the Western Powers that the veto should not be used except as a last resort, and then only to protect the vital interests of a Great Power from being threatened by a majority vote of the Council. The Russians, however, used it to obstruct any action of which they happened to disapprove. They blocked the admission of a number of law-abiding States to the United Nations; they prevented the United Nations from taking any effective part in bringing an end to the Greek civil war; they opposed all measures to bring armaments, and especially the manufacture of atomic bombs, under rigorous international control.

It was on this last point that the Russian attitude most deeply shocked American public opinion. The United States government had proposed in June 1946 to the United Nations Atomic Energy Committee a plan (known as the Baruch Plan) to put all phases of the development and control of atomic energy under an international authority which would have "managerial control and ownership of all atomic energy activities potentially dangerous to world security" and which would have "power to control, inspect and license all other atomic activities." To this authority the United States would surrender "full information as to the know-how for the production of atomic energy," and as soon as it was in full working order the existing stocks of bombs would be disposed of and all manufacture of bombs would stop. The Plan added that "there must be no veto to protect those who violate their solemn agreements not to develop or use atomic energy for destructive purposes."

As the Americans and many other people saw it, the Baruch Plan was an essential foundation for world peace. Here was a nation which was in sole possession of the new weapon and of the means for its production offering to sacrifice its advantage. The Russian refusal to accept the proposal in any form unless it were so modified as to rule out any real inspection or control awoke the Western world to the difficulties, if not to the actual unlikelihood, of a joint peace settlement.

PERSIA, TURKEY AND GREECE

The fifth front on which Russian policy came into collision with that of the Western Powers was in Persia, Turkey and Greece. The Persian situation should have left no room for misunderstanding. An Anglo-Soviet-Persian agreement signed in January 1942 had established a Russian zone of occupation in the north of Persia and a British zone in the south, Teheran being in the joint occupation of the Soviet Union and Britain. It was laid down that all foreign troops would leave the country within six months of the end of the war. But long before the war ended it became obvious that the Russians were trying to separate their zone from the rest of Persia. The world was told that Persian Azerbaijan wished to become incorporated in the Azerbaijan Soviet Republic of the U.S.S.R. In 1945 the Russians were showing no intention of withdrawing their troops. The United States tried to set an example by withdrawing American troops in November, but this was unavailing, as was also a Persian appeal to the Security Council in January 1946. The situation looked increasingly ugly, until suddenly in May the Soviet Union for no appreciable reason abandoned its position and withdrew its troops from Persia.

In Turkey the Russians had no troops but they lost no time in making claims on Turkish territory. The provinces of Kars and Ardahan, it was said, were historically Russian and should be handed over to the Soviet Union. This was a threat rather than a serious or official claim. What was serious was the Soviet government's demand that the Montreux Agreement on the Black Sea Straits should be superseded by an agreement negotiated separately between Turkey and the Soviet Union. The Russians were anxious to have military installations on Turkish territory overlooking the Straits.

From the point of view of Russian security this was very reasonable. Russia's most vulnerable point, now that Eastern Europe was covered, lay in the regions of the southern Ukraine and the Transcaucasian oilfields. Any buffer between these areas and the outside world would have been welcome. Persian Azerbaijan and Turkish Kars and Ardahan were desirable, but control of the Black Sea Straits might well seem essential. It had been a Russian ambition for at least two centuries. Britain had had no hesitation in promising it to tsarist Russia during the First World War. Why could she not promise it to Soviet Russia during the second? After all, Britain controlled two of the three outlets to the Mediterranean: why should she object to Russia's controlling the third, which was much more vital to Russia's interests than were Gibraltar or Suez to Britain? To Britain and the United States, on the other hand, Russian ambitions in the Black Sea Straits and

the Aegean savored of naked aggrandizement. They supported Turkey's refusal to discuss changes in the Montreux
Agreement tête-à-tête with the Soviet Union.

In Greece the Soviet Union made no claim and seemed to
have taken no interest. Stalin had shown no hesitation in
agreeing to Churchill's suggestion in October 1944 that the
Russians should deal with the Rumanians and Bulgarians and
that the British should deal with the Greeks. When British
troops put down the rising of the Greek Communists, he did
not object. As Churchill admitted in his *Second World War*,
"Stalin however adhered strictly and faithfully to our agreement of October, and during all the long weeks of fighting
the Communists in the streets of Athens not one word of
reproach came from *Pravda* and *Izvestia*." But when Com-
munist-controlled governments were established on Greece's
northern frontiers, the Russian attitude changed. The Greek
Communists were now advised by Moscow and had support
in Yugoslavia, Bulgaria and Albania, from which countries
they were drawing ammunition and supplies in 1946 for raising a new army to attempt to wreck the Greek economy and
political regime so precariously established by the British.
This threat forced the British government into commitments
it felt unable to meet. In February 1947 it informed the
United States State Department that "economic necessity
dictated the relinquishment of British financial and military
burdens in Greece as from the end of the current financial
year, that is to say, in precisely five weeks' time."

The American President's answer to this came on March
12, when he asked Congress for $400 million for the help of
Greece and Turkey, declaring that "it must be the policy of
the United States to support free peoples who are resisting
attempted subjugation by armed minorities or by outside
pressure."

This declaration, which became known as the Truman Doctrine, was the first open breach between Russia and the United States. To the Russians it could seem nothing but menacing. Here were the Americans interesting themselves for the first time in two countries which commanded access from the Mediterranean to the Ukraine and the Transcaucasian oil-fields — to the "soft underbelly" of the Soviet Union. And the Truman Doctrine was proclaimed at the very moment when the Council of Foreign Ministers was opening its most important conference in Moscow. Such timing, thought the Russians, was surely a threat.

It was not surprising that the Moscow Conference merely widened the gulf between the Eastern and Western allies and brought nearer the breakdown of the policy of joint settlement. Molotov claimed huge reparations from Germany and insisted that they should be taken not only in capital equipment but out of current production. George Marshall and Ernest Bevin, representing the United States and Great Britain, referred to the Potsdam Agreement and declared themselves opposed "to allowing Russia to take income out of Germany at one end, while they were priming the pump at the other end to the extent of $700 million a year." There was a long debate on the political constitution of Germany, which the Russians wanted to be a centralized state while the Americans and British preferred a federal structure. (Here Molotov was on firmer ground, for the Germans were opposed to federalism. What he sought to gain by a centralized Germany was Communist control of the central government.) But before the political constitution of Germany could be adumbrated, the frontiers must be decided, and here again there was disagreement, the Russians claiming that the Oder-Neisse frontier in the east had been determined, while the Western Powers pointed out that, as laid down in the Potsdam Agreement, it was a matter for the final peace settlement. Even over Germany's western frontier, Bidault, the French Foreign Minister, wanted international control of the Ruhr and the separation of the Rhineland from Germany. None of the other members of the Council would concede the latter point, and the British and Americans were opposed to him on the former. The Moscow Conference broke up on April 24 with nothing decided except that the Foreign Ministers would meet again in London in November.

THE MARSHALL OFFER

In the meantime the course of international politics was changed by a surprising offer made by the American Secretary of State and by an even more surprising reaction to it on the part of European governments. In a speech at Harvard on June 5, 1947, George Marshall said: "The truth of the matter is that Europe's requirements for the next three or four years of foreign food and other essential products — principally from America — are so much greater than her present ability to pay that she must have substantial additional help or face economic, social and physical deterioration of a very grave character. It is logical that the United States should do whatever it is able to do to assist in the return of normal economic health in the world, without which there can be no political stability and no assured peace." In other words the United States had recognized the implications of its role as the world's richest power and was prepared to finance not only the relief but the recovery of Europe.

General Marshall added: "The initiative, I think, must come from Europe. The role of this country should consist of friendly aid in the drafting of a European program and of later support of such a program as far as it may be practicable for us to do so. The program should be a joint one, agreed

to by a number of, if not all, European nations." The initiative was in fact taken immediately by the British and French
governments, who proposed to the Russian government a
meeting between their three Foreign Ministers, and Bevin,
Bidault and Molotov met in Paris on June 27.

Here was the most dramatic opportunity since Potsdam
nearly two years ago for cementing a joint peace settlement.
If the European states were to combine to draw up a European recovery program on the basis of economic collaboration
among themselves and financial assistance from the United
States, the essential foundations for joint settlement would
be laid.

The Russians had a difficult decision to make. Were the
Marshall Plan to succeed, they could ill afford to keep out
of it; were it to fail, it would be better for them to keep their
hands clear of it from the start. They believed that it would
break down. The Kremlin view at that time was that financial
collapse in the capitalist world was not only inevitable but
likely to be immediate. So Molotov temporized at Paris,
and when the British and French governments invited twenty-
two other European countries to a conference on the Marshall
offer in July, the Soviet Union forbade the states under her
influence to attend. Poland, Hungary, Yugoslavia, Rumania,
Bulgaria and Albania had to stay away; so had Finland and
Czechoslovakia, though they had shown a desire to attend.

Thus the postwar division of Europe was marked clearly
for the first time. The Russians had evidently decided that
they could not risk joint settlement with the Western Powers
on any plane. It had become obvious that their policy was
to concentrate on obtaining security through the control of
a ring of satellite nations (see Chapter 5). The Western
Powers had now to recognize that they must have a new
policy. For two whole years after the defeat of Germany the

governments of the West had acted on the assumption that, given patience and forbearance, a general peace settlement could be made jointly with the Soviet Union. The United States had shown confidence by disarming — her armed forces were reduced from nearly twelve million men in 1945 to one and a half million in 1947 — and by allowing the greater part of the money voted to UNRRA (the United Nations Relief and Rehabilitation Administration) to go to the Soviet Union and to Russian-controlled countries. Britain's confidence was shown not only in disarmament — reducing her armed forces from over five million to less than one and a half million — but also in her refusal to do anything in the British zone of occupation in Germany which might antagonize the Soviet Union. It was now realized that that confidence had been misplaced. The Conference of Foreign Ministers, meeting in London in November and December 1947 confirmed that realization: Molotov would agree with the other Foreign Ministers on nothing whatever.

CHAPTER 3

THE POLICY OF CONTAINMENT

A CHAPTER IN HISTORY ended with the year 1947. In 1948 the Western Powers inaugurated a new policy to take the place of the abortive joint settlement. It was to be known as the policy of Containment. In essence it was an attempt to prevent the further expansion of Russian influence and control by organizing the non-Communist countries of Europe on military, economic and political levels, while keeping the door open to Russian admission to these organizations in the event of a change of policy in the Kremlin. It would mean rearmament and would involve the obvious danger that Russia might strike before the West was strong. It would mean recognizing that the Great Powers were divided into two armed camps and postponing all hopes of a general peace settlement. But to the Western world after 1947 there seemed to be no alternative.

The first stage in the policy of Containment concerned Germany. Britain and the United States had undertaken the economic fusion of their zones in 1946, but it had led to no economic recovery because any approach to the essential currency reform was blocked by the Russians. Now there would

have to be a new currency in the western zones, however
much that might divide West and East Germany. Further,
there would have to be a political fusion of the British, American and French zones which would lead to the establishment
of a West German republic in alliance with the Western
Powers. All this would take time, but if there were any doubts
in Western minds about its urgency, they were ended by a
startling Communist riposte.

On February 25, 1948, the world learned to its astonish-
ment that a predominantly Communist government had been
established in Czechoslovakia. Only nine months ago President Beneš had proclaimed that Czechoslovakia "was a truly
democratic and socialist State, choosing neither the Russian
system nor the American liberalistic system," and in Western
eyes Czechoslovakia was still a parliamentary democracy, be-
longing to Western Europe in culture and civilization though
linked to Russia by Slav racial bonds and by fear of Germany.
What happened in February was that the Czech Minister of
the Interior, a Communist, dismissed eight police chiefs in
Prague, intending to replace them by Communists, where-
upon a majority of the Cabinet objected and eleven of them
handed in their resignation. The Czech Communist Party —
guided, it may be, by Zorin, a deputy Foreign Minister of the
Soviet Union who happened to be visiting Prague — now
went into action. The police and many trade unions were
on their side. President Beneš had to give way and accept
a Communist government. The West had to recognize that
Czechoslovakia was now firmly and finally part of the Soviet
bloc. It was a great triumph for the Kremlin, which had won
Czechoslovakia's accession without sending a single unit of
the Red Army into the country and without — as far as anyone could prove — a single threat.

REVIVING WESTERN GERMANY

The Western Powers now rushed through the currency reform in Germany. It had been long prepared — the Americans had a plan ready for their zone as early as May 1946 — and only the desire not to antagonize the Russians and not to separate the east and west of Germany had held it up. In June 1948 it was put into effect. Lucius D. Clay notes in his book *Decision in Germany*:

> The immediate effect of the currency reform was startling. As soon as it went into operation Director of Economics Erhard had, I think wisely, removed price and rationing controls except on food, fuel, steel, rent, essential clothing and a few other very scarce items. Immediately goods and raw materials came out of hiding. Shop windows and shelves filled up with goods and production lines increased overnight as hoarded raw materials were rushed to process. Of course an immediate buying spree resulted. A consumer-starved population rushed to spend its new marks.

By the end of the year, "Internally the situation had improved beyond belief. Food and consumer goods were meeting the demand. . . . There was a new bustle in German life, new life and courage in German faces."

To the Russians the introduction of the new currency in the Western zones was a severe blow. They had their riposte ready. The three Western Powers each held sectors in Berlin where they were responsible for a civilian population of about 2,500,000 people. But Berlin was in the center of the Russian zone: the Russians could deny access to the city by road, rail and canal. In that case, they reckoned, the Western Powers would be unable to feed the Germans in their sectors of Berlin and would have to evacuate the capital. The effect of that would be loss of confidence in the Western Powers throughout western Germany: the economic revival would be nipped in the bud and all plans for a West German government would be stillborn.

The Russian blockade of Berlin began on June 24. General Clay wrote that "it was one of the most ruthless efforts in modern times to use mass starvation for political coercion. Our food stocks on hand were sufficient to last for thirty-six days and our coal-stocks for forty-five." The Anglo-American answer was an airlift. Operation Vittles, as the Americans called it, flew food, clothing, coal, raw materials and medicines into the Western sectors of Berlin. Thanks in part to a winter free from severe snow or fog, the airlift was a success. By the spring of 1949 a daily average of 8000 tons was being flown in. On May 11 the Russians lifted the blockade. Their Berlin riposte had been as much of a failure as the Prague coup was a success.

Besides saving the Berliners from starvation, the airlift convinced Germans in the Western zones that the United States and Britain had their interests at heart and were strong enough to secure them. Public opinion was now behind the formation of a West German state, even though it would postpone the reunification of Germany which, in one form or another, was the heart's desire of every German. The constitution of that state, the German Federal Republic, was signed in Bonn in May 1949.

THE MILITARY ALLIANCES

Meanwhile the Western Powers had been building up their policy of Containment on the military level. The first stage was the Brussels Treaty signed in March 1948 by Britain, France, Belgium, the Netherlands and Luxembourg. In striking contrast to the Dunkirk Treaty of alliance between Britain and France signed twelve months earlier, which was aimed at defense against Germany ("Should either of the High Contracting Parties become again involved in hostilities with Germany . . ."), the Brussels Treaty looked farther afield ("If any of the High Contracting Parties should be the object of an armed attack in Europe . . ."). The Brussels Treaty was an innovation in that it set up a permanent organization for carrying its provisions into effect; there were to be not only a Consultative Council of Foreign Ministers of the signatory powers, a Permanent Commission of Ambassadors in London and a Defense Committee of Defense Ministers, but also military committees and commanders of the joint land, sea and air forces. Never had an alliance achieved such close integration in time of peace.

It was obvious that the Brussels Powers, however closely integrated, would be unable to withstand a full-scale attack by the Soviet Union. Without the assured support in arms of the United States and Canada, military containment could be little but bluff. That support was secured by the North Atlantic Treaty signed on April 4, 1949, by the five Brussels Powers, the United States, Canada, Italy, Iceland, Norway, Denmark and Portugal (Greece and Turkey were to add their signatures in 1952). The combined armed forces of these Powers were vastly inferior in number to those of the U.S.S.R. At the end of the war the Western Allies had nearly 20 million men under arms; in 1949 the number had sunk to less than 3 million, while the Soviet Union still had armed forces of over 4 million and an air force at its wartime strength of 20,000 planes. But the atomic bomb was still an American monopoly, and under cover of the tacit threat of its use the North Atlantic Powers would have time to rearm.

The North Atlantic Treaty was an innovation in more ways

than one. It was the first formal military alliance to which the United States had committed itself since 1778. It was the widest military commitment which Britain had ever made. "The Parties agree that an armed attack against one or more of them in Europe or North America shall be an attack against them all": this undertaking (in Article V) meant that Britain, for instance, would be involved in war if the Soviet Union were to attack Norway or Turkey, its immediate neighbors. It involved a permanent organization both fuller and more extended than that set up under the Brussels Treaty. The North Atlantic Treaty Organization (NATO), which absorbed the Brussels Treaty Organization, employed an international staff of officials and service officers and set up in Paris a Supreme Headquarters of Allied Powers in Europe (SHAPE) and a corresponding command in Norfolk, Virginia, covering the North Atlantic Ocean, to control all land, sea and air operations in the event of war.

ECONOMIC AND POLITICAL CO-ORDINATION

On the economic level collaboration did not go nearly as far, but the efforts made for the restoration of European economy far surpassed anything foreseen at the time of Marshall's Harvard speech in June 1947. Russia and her allies had excluded themselves from the Marshall Plan, but the other European states, meeting in a Committee for European Economic Co-operation, produced an estimate in September 1947 of the dollars needed for their economic recovery. In the 1948 atmosphere of the Prague coup and the Berlin blockade the United States Congress was much more inclined to vote the sums needed than it would have been at any other time since the war. The European Recovery Program was being transformed into the economic aspect of the policy of Con-

tainment. Congress voted $4000 million for Europe for the
year beginning April 1948, and an Organization for European
Economic Co-operation representative of all the participating
countries was set up to achieve "a sound European economy
through the co-operation of its members." The O.E.E.C.
agreed to apportion the dollars among its members in such
a way that Britain received about a quarter and France about
a fifth of the total aid.

A movement for the political union of Western Europe
had been gathering way ever since thoughts had first turned
to postwar reconstruction. In Italy, France and the Low
Countries there was a widespread belief, especially among the
younger generation, that without union Western Europe
would not be able to support itself, defend itself or preserve
its civilization. Americans were strongly and impatiently of
the opinion that the European states should form a federation
on the lines, more or less, of the United States. The movement was precipitated in 1948 by the fear of Russia. Winston
Churchill was the inspiration of a congress of unofficial bodies
which met at The Hague in May to make propaganda for
Western union. The Brussels Powers set up an official committee in November to consider a European Assembly. Out
of all this emerged the Council of Europe, with its seat in
Strasbourg.

The members of the Council of Europe were the European states who belonged to NATO, with the addition of
Switzerland, Sweden, Portugal, and Austria and, later, of the
Federal Republic of western Germany. Its organs were a
Council of Ministers, a Consultative Assembly consisting of
delegates from the parliaments of each of the member states
and an international secretariat. The Assembly had no legislative powers; it was essentially a forum where European public
opinion could be formed and expressed. It alone could pro-

vide the embryo of a European parliament, for the O.E.E.C. was an inter-governmental body deliberating in secret, and NATO was not a European organization. A great debate animated the Council in its early years, a debate between federalists, led by the French, who wanted to proceed immediately to a federal constitution of non-Communist Europe, and the pragmatists, who preferred to approach political union deviously and gradually by way of organizations for limited and practical purposes.

By the middle of 1949 the Western Powers could feel highly satisfied with their policy of Containment. Russia's blockade of Berlin, broken by the airlift, had been ended. Western Germany was finding its feet economically and was on its way to forming a Federal Republic under a democratic government. Russia had added Czechoslovakia to the company of Kremlin-controlled states, but she had lost Yugoslavia, whose leader, Tito, had broken with Stalin and was to prove strong enough to steer Yugoslavia on an independent course. Russia had failed, too, in Greece, where the long and devastating civil war ended in 1948 with the defeat of the Communists. The United States had made a success of the Marshall Plan, which was putting wind into the economic sails of Europe from Norway to Turkey. And the North Atlantic Treaty Organization had been launched.

But then suddenly the Western Powers had to realize that the policy of Containment involved not simply containing Communist Russia in Europe but in Asia as well. China, the most populous nation in the world, was coming under Communist control. In September 1949 the People's Republic was proclaimed. By the end of the year the whole of China was in the hands of the Communist Party under Mao Tsetung (see Part II, Chapter 6). On February 14, 1950, a Sino-Soviet treaty of friendship, alliance and mutual assistance was signed. What it would mean for Russia and China to be in league under Communist governments was soon to be shown in Korea.

THE KOREAN WAR

Since the expulsion of the Japanese, Korea had been in the charge of the Soviet Union and the United States, their respective zones of military occupation being divided by the 38th parallel of latitude. It was a purely artificial line, corresponding to no geographical, economic or social division in Korea, and was not intended to be lasting. Korea was a single nation with a history of a thousand years of independence; the only purpose of the occupation was to remove traces of Japanese conquest and to set Korea up as a united, democratic and sovereign State. But the Russians naturally wanted Korea to be united under a Communist regime friendly to the Soviet Union, and the Americans equally naturally wanted it to be united under a non-Communist regime friendly to the United States. By September 1947 they had still reached no agreement and the United States referred the question to the Assembly of the United Nations, which sent a UN Temporary Commission to Korea. This Commission was boycotted by the Russians and their nominees in the north; all it could do was to recommend that elections should be held in South Korea. As far as it could see, these elections, which were held in May 1948, were "a valid expression of the free will of the people." They resulted in a National Assembly which elected Syngman Rhee as President. The Russians countered by setting up a People's Democratic Republic under Communist control in the north.

The position now was that two rival governments, each claiming control of all Korea, were facing each other across

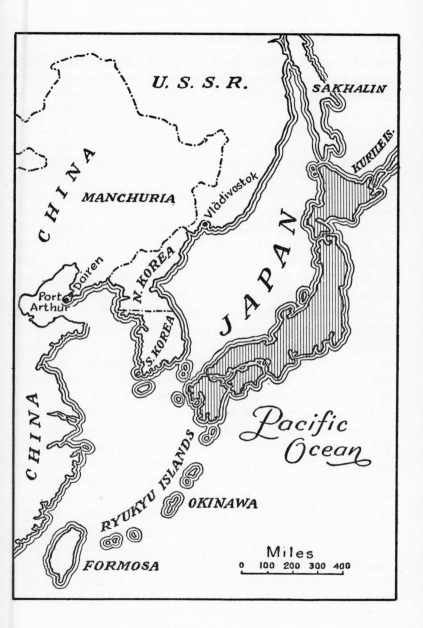

U. S. S. R.

SAKHALIN

KURILE IS.

CHINA

MANCHURIA

Vladivostok

JAPAN

Dairen

N. KOREA

Port Arthur

S. KOREA

CHINA

Pacific Ocean

RYUKYU ISLANDS

OKINAWA

FORMOSA

Miles
0   100   200   300   400

the 38th parallel, with the rival backing of the United States
and the Soviet Union. The Russians felt enough confidence
in their protégés to remove Russian troops from the north by
the end of 1948; the Americans could not in decency postpone the removal of their forces from the south after the
middle of 1949. The next twelve months were loud in the
expression of aggressive intentions by the rival Korean governments, and on June 25, 1950, full-scale armed aggression was
started by the Communist government of the north, which
sent its troops across the line.

On paper it was a civil war between Koreans; in fact it was
a piece of aggression by proxy by the Soviet Union. The Russians had everything to gain by the war and nothing to lose.
If their North Korean protégés were to win, Russia would
be in control of the whole North Pacific coastline of Asia from
the Arctic to Port Arthur, and by adding South Korean bases
to the airfields in the Kuriles and South Sakhalin the Russian
semi-encirclement of Japan would be complete. If they were
to lose, neither Russian arms nor Russian prestige would be
directly involved, and there would always be propaganda
capital to be made out of the misdoings of the victors.

The United Nations took immediate action. There was
no question of a Communist veto on the Security Council,
for the Soviet Union had withdrawn its representatives in
January 1950 and China was represented by the government
of Chiang Kai-shek. The Council called for the immediate
withdrawal of North Korean forces from territory south of
the 38th parallel. When this was ignored, American armed
support was sent to the government of the south. It came
just in time to prevent the whole peninsula from being overrun by the North Korean Communists. By October the
Americans were in sufficient force to drive the aggressors back
across the 38th parallel and northward to the Chinese border

in Manchuria. But then the whole complexion of the war was changed by the intervention of Communist China. By the end of the year Chinese forces had pushed the UN contingents back into South Korea and the "Korean incident" had turned into a full-scale if strictly localized war. It was not only a war of Koreans against Koreans but of Chinese using Russian planes and equipment against Americans helped by contingents of their fellow members of the United Nations.

Until April 1951 the front was fluid; then it was stabilized on or about the 38th parallel. Long-drawn-out truce negotiations ended in an armistice signed in July 1953. The war thus ended in stalemate with the Korean problem no nearer solution than it had been before the fighting began. The Western Powers could feel that they had succeeded in "containing" Communism on the Korean front. The Chinese under Mao Tse-tung could be happy in having secured a Communist buffer on the Korean side of their Manchurian frontier, even though the Korean War had led the Americans to give the protection of their fleet to Formosa in support of Chiang Kai-shek, whom they still recognized as head of the government of China. But the greatest satisfaction was Russia's. The war had cost her nothing and had made the Chinese Communists realize their dependence on Russian arms and supplies; it had strengthened the Moscow-Peking axis. The people who could feel no satisfaction at all were the Koreans. Their country had been devastated and perhaps 3 million of their 30 million population had been killed (American losses were 25,000 dead; British 600).

CONTAINING CHINA

Containment of Russia, it was now realized, must mean the containment of China as well. Not that the Chinese Communists were being overtly aggressive. They had not entered the Korean War until United Nations forces had reached their Manchurian frontier and American generals were openly talking of bombing Chinese installations in Manchuria. But as the first strong and centralized government that China had had for centuries their tone was bellicose; and their action in Tibet, if not technically aggressive, was anything but reassuring.

Tibet had legally been part of the old Chinese Empire and the Chinese Republic had never given up the claim to suzerainty. In fact Tibet had remained independent, an unknown country lost behind the mountains, its frontiers not fixed because they had never been fully surveyed. In 1950 Mao Tse-tung sent an expedition to Tibet to establish Chinese rule. It was a remarkable expedition: less than 30,000 troops, with equipment including jeeps dropped by parachute, motor trucks which were often taken to pieces, carried by hand and reassembled, and rations more familiar to an Everest expedition than to an army. Only a quarter of this force was lost by natural causes — cold, starvation, fever and disappearance. The survivors reached Lhasa, and within a year of the invasion the Tibetan army and the whole of the country were under their control. The successful military invasion was followed by an act of political patience. The Dalai Lama was reinstalled in dignity in Lhasa and traditional Tibetan life was only slowly modified.

A more dangerous direction for China's expansion was toward the south, where Chinese had emigrated and multiplied exceedingly. There were four million Chinese in Siam and three million in Malaya and Singapore. The land link between China and Siam and Malaya lay through French Indochina, where a war had been in progress since 1946 between the French and the Vietnamese nationalists (see Part II, Chapter

5). When the Chinese Communists reached the Indochinese frontier at the beginning of 1950 it was only natural that they should supply arms and equipment to the Vietnamese leader, Ho Chi Minh, himself a Communist, who was fighting the French imperialists. The Soviet Union joined Communist China in recognizing Ho Chi Minh as ruler of Vietnam in January 1950. When the French failed to hold Ho Chi Minh's force in northern Vietnam and the United States was prevailed upon to send assistance in the form of supplies and equipment, it looked as though a war of the Korean type would develop in Indochina. In the autumn of 1954, while Ho Chi Minh's armies were assembling for an attack on Hanoi which the French could hardly hope to resist, an international conference was held at Geneva, attended not only by representatives of the protagonists but by Molotov and Chou En-lai on behalf of the great Communist Powers and by Eden and Dulles representing Britain and the United States. A truce was arranged on the Korean pattern, leaving Vietnam north of the 17th parallel of latitude to Ho Chi Minh, while the French Expeditionary Corps remained in the south. It was declared that elections would be held in the whole of Vietnam in July 1956 to decide the future of the country.

The question still was: Where and how could Containment be applied to Asia? The southern Asiatic peoples were not impassioned by the rivalry between the Great Powers. They were not convinced of the aggressive intention of Russia or of China, or if they were, they could not be persuaded that armed opposition was the best policy. India, the only southern Asian power with considerable armed forces and armaments, took up a position of neutrality. If the United States and the British Commonwealth insisted on containing Communism by military force, they would have to provide it themselves.

At a conference at Manila in September 1954 Dulles, the United States Secretary of State, succeeded in getting agreement to the setting up of a Southeast Asia Treaty Organization (SEATO). This was carried a stage further at a conference in Bangkok in February 1955, when the eight SEATO Powers (the United States, Britain, France, Australia, New Zealand, Pakistan, Siam, the Philippines) established a Permanent Council with a secretariat in the Siamese capital.

INTEGRATING WESTERN EUROPE

The fact that the danger points in the Great Power rivalry in the early 1950's were in the Far East did not make any less pressing the need of each side to make sure of as much of Germany as possible. The Russians intensified economic control of their zone, now dignified by the title of German Democratic Republic, and built up a military police which was to all intents and purposes an army. The Western Powers, which were now dealing with an increasingly independent German government at Bonn, had to move more cautiously. From France came the most original idea, envisaging a supranational organization for the control of coal and steel, Europe's basic industries. It was proposed by Robert Schuman, France's Foreign Minister, in May 1950, and when Britain, to his vast disappointment, refused to join, it was founded by a treaty signed by the states of "Little Europe" (France, Holland, Belgium, Luxembourg, West Germany and Italy) in April 1951. The Coal-and-Steel Community was intended to be the basis of a political federation, but by 1955 it had got no farther than creating a common market for coal and steel, abolishing tariffs and quotas in these commodities throughout Little Europe.

The idea of a military community also came from France.

When at the height of the Korean crisis in 1950 the American Secretary of State announced that it was his government's desire that Western Germany should be rearmed so as to take part in the defense of the West against Russian aggression, Pleven, the French Prime Minister, replied by proposing a European Defense Community with a European army to which every member state would contribute a part of its armed forces. In this partnership, the French believed, Germany would be useful but harmless to the West. Germany's armed forces would all go under the supra-national control of the E.D.C., whereas the other members would retain part if not most of their national forces under their own State control. Even in the European Army the German force would, according to the Pleven Plan of 1950, be a comparatively small element and not in the command of German officers except at a very low level.

Changing circumstances made the French lose their enthusiasm for the E.D.C. Britain refused to join it, thus facing France with the uncomfortable prospect of being left alone with Germany as a major partner in the Community. The Germans, realizing that the United States was intent on their rearmament against Soviet Russia, bargained for a stronger position in the European Army. When, after two years of negotiation, the E.D.C. treaty was at last signed, an immediate attack by Russia was no longer feared, and there was nothing but American pressure to make the French Assembly feel that it need ratify the treaty. The European Army by then seemed a very different thing. Instead of involving only a fraction of the French armed forces while the greater part remained under French sovereignty, it would clearly involve all and possibly more than all that France could spare for European fronts now that the war in Indochina was absorbing her military energies.

The French Assembly rejected the E.D.C. treaty in July 1954. After a flurry of diplomatic activity, the Western Powers reached a new agreement on German rearmament in the autumn. This recognized West Germany's right to rearm while limiting her forces to twelve divisions and excluding her from the right to manufacture atomic, bacteriological and chemical weapons. It brought West Germany into the Brussels Treaty and into NATO, while allaying French fears by the provision that Britain, unless prevented by a "serious overseas emergency," would continue to maintain in arms on the continent of Europe four divisions (120,000 men) and a tactical air force. The new agreement was called Western European Union, but by 1955 it had not got far in that direction. It was a further step in the policy of Containment, though not yet an effective step, for the Germans in the Federal Republic were still unmobilized and unarmed. Ten years after the war a peace settlement of Germany seemed far away. The great nation had recovered economically but was partitioned and still occupied by the forces of rival foreign powers.

In the spring of 1955 there was a *détente*. Arrangements were made for a meeting of heads of governments, the first since Potsdam in 1945. The Russians made a concession to Western opinion by signing jointly with the Western Powers a treaty with Austria in which they modified their previous claims: all occupying forces would be removed from the Republic and the Russians would retain no property rights in Austria, which would pay to the Soviet Union about £715,000 for the Danubian Steamship Company and would deliver goods to the total value of £50 million in addition to one million tons of crude oil annually for the next ten years. At last it seemed as if the time had come to revise the policy of Containment, the military strategy of which had been based on the assumption of Western superiority in nuclear weapons, an assumption which could no longer be held with certainty now that the Soviet Union was producing not only atomic but also hydrogen bombs.

Summer saw the Russians in even more smiling mood. In June the Soviet Prime Minister and the Secretary General of the Communist Party paid a visit to Yugoslavia, apologized for all the bitter words that had been said against Tito since 1948 (see page 76) and signed a declaration with him recognizing that different countries might reach the goal of socialism by different ways. In July the heads of government — Eisenhower, Bulganin, Faure and Eden — met in Geneva with an agenda on which the main items were the reunification of Germany, disarmament and contacts between East and West. The Russians showed no intention of allowing the reunification of Germany on any terms except their own, or of permitting any supervision of disarmament, and what they meant by contacts was trade with the West, whereas what the West meant was freer circulation of individuals. What the Russians really wanted was NATO's abandonment of its bases; what the other Powers really wanted was the relaxation of Russia's grip on Central and Eastern Europe. Neither side would yield, and no agreement was reached at Geneva, but at least the atmosphere of the Conference had been not unfriendly and way to negotiation had been opened.

In September the Russians still seemed to be conciliatory. They recognized the German Federal Republic, after entertaining its Chancellor, Dr. Adenauer, in Moscow. They relinquished their lease of Porkkala and undertook to hand it back to Finland. But the impression of good intentions which these gestures made was canceled in the eyes of the West by the news that the Soviet government had been arranging for the sale of Czechoslovakian armaments to Egypt and intending thus to pursue an active policy in the Arab world, an area in which they had not hitherto intervened.

CHAPTER 4

RECOVERY IN FRANCE AND ITALY

THE DEFEAT AND occupation of Germany meant that — apart from Russia — France and Italy were the only two powers left in continental Europe with any pretensions to greatness. Both had suffered so severely during the war that the possibility of recovery after 1945 seemed extremely doubtful.

France had been sorely stricken. Economically her losses were nothing in comparison with those of Germany, but they were serious enough. Two million of her people had been imprisoned. According to Antoine Pinay:

> Property amounting to 55,000 factories and business houses, 135,000 agricultural buildings, and 2,000,000 dwelling-houses was destroyed or damaged . . . more than 4000 kilometres of railways and more than 7500 bridges were destroyed. To realize the magnitude of these disasters, and I refer only to complete destruction, it is necessary to visualize the disappearance from the map of France of a department as large and as well populated as that of the Nord, or the devastation of three-quarters of the city of Paris. . . . At the liberation industrial production was only one-half of that of 1938.

The political damage seemed more difficult to repair than the economic. The Third Republic had disintegrated under defeat by the Germans in 1940. The Vichy regime under Marshal Pétain which succeeded it had been swept away by the Anglo-American invasion and the French resistance movement in 1944. The government of France was in the hands of General de Gaulle and a coalition of ministers representing the main resistance groups, including the Communists, but it was October 1945 before Britain could bring herself to recognize this, and at the Potsdam Conference France was not represented.

Morally the damage was most serious of all. France had been defeated in 1940, and in defeat her record was not glorious. Frenchmen had been divided against Frenchmen, some collaborating more or less willingly with the Nazi German conquerors, some resisting more or less gallantly. It seemed to many observers that the disgrace of 1940 had gone too deep and that cleavage between collaborators and resisters had become too acute for the recovery and unity of France to be possible. But this pessimism proved unjustified. The disgrace was forgotten, the cleavage healed. A few of the more outrageous collaborators — Laval among them — were put to death, but only a few; there was surprisingly little vindictiveness. Instead of moral degeneration there was in 1945 a sense of liberation and renaissance. As Dorothy M. Pickles wrote in *French Politics*, "There was, for a short time, a sincere spirit of moral and social purpose, of unity and brotherly love, a sense of democratic rebirth which set up Wordsworthian reactions in more than one British observer whose feet were normally planted firmly on the ground."

This spirit was reflected by the Provisional Government under De Gaulle and was illustrated by the results of the first postwar general elections which were held in October

1945. Instead of the myriad ill-organized parties into which French Assemblies had traditionally been divided, more than three-quarters of the members returned to the new Constitutional Assembly were either Communists, Socialists or members of the M.R.P. The Communists owed their votes partly to their record in the Resistance, in which after June 1941 they had been most rabidly anti-German, the Socialists to the prospect which they together with the Communists offered of radical social reform, and the M.R.P. (*Mouvement Républicain Populaire*), a new party, to the fact that it stood — with Resistance leaders such as Georges Bidault and Maurice Schumann at its head — for a policy which would be both Socialist and Catholic.

A coalition of these three parties under the leadership of General de Gaulle gave France a number of lasting reforms, including State control of the Bank of France, of the four big credit banks and of the Renault works and the nationalization of the gas industry, the electricity industry and the major insurance companies. But the unity could not last. The General could not for long drive a team which included the Communists; he resigned in January 1946. The three parties could not agree on the nature of the new constitution and became more concerned with electioneering than with governing. Between May and November 1946 there were two elections and two referendums before the constitution of the Fourth Republic was accepted and an Assembly elected under its terms.

In calling the new regime the Fourth Republic, Frenchmen meant to show that they intended it to be different from the Third. In fact it turned out to be very much the same. Governments were still coalitions of parties and personalities at odds with each other and at the mercy of the Assembly. They fell as frequently as those of the Third and were as little able to pursue firm, long-term policies. As time went on and the enthusiasm of the Liberation period waned, the radicals and the Right-wing parties of the Third Republic revived, and of the three big parties of 1945–46 only the Communists retained their electoral support.

COMMUNISTS, GAULLISTS AND THIRD FORCE

Five million French men and women (French women had been given the vote for the first time in 1945) continued to vote Communist at every election in the postwar decade. Why, one can only guess; no one can ever know why electors vote as they do. It was not that there was much Communism in France either in the sense of loyalty to theoretical Marxism or in that of approval of the actions of the Bolsheviks in Russia or of their puppets in Eastern Europe. It was rather that five million French electors had grievances which in their belief only the Communists could remove: the high food prices, the shocking housing shortage, and the wide disparity between the standards of living of the rich and the poor all cried out for swift reforms which no other party could so well convince the electorate of its determination to undertake. The effectiveness of the propaganda of the Communists made all the other French parties look stupid. After the Liberation, when so many Frenchmen had bad consciences about collaboration, the Communists were able to pose as the anti-Fascist party, as the party *par excellence* of Democracy. After the failure of the Moscow Conference, when the prospect of a third world war began to loom, they were the party of Peace. After the collapse of successive Leftist coalition governments, they were the party which stood for the working class when the rest had failed. Throughout the postwar decade they were able to appeal to trade unionists sufficiently to control the

C.G.T., which remained the largest trade union organization.

Their propaganda was even more intelligent in detail than in general. In the industrial northeast the slogan would be "Cheap Food"; in the agricultural south, it would be "Higher Food Prices." A constituency of peasant farmers would be promised private property in land and no death duties; a constituency of employees would be promised precisely the opposite. In France, where a member of parliament is expected to be a local beneficiary, the inconsistencies were not disturbing. The Frenchman likes to vote for politicians who profess a broad political principle and act in a narrow parochial interest. The Communists succeeded in combining the two.

General de Gaulle saw the answer to the strength of the Communists and the feebleness of the other parties in a rally of all Frenchmen who stood for strong, patriotic government. For this purpose he founded the R.P.F. (Rassemblement du Peuple Français) in April 1947. He intended it to be a movement cutting across party lines, but it soon turned into a Right-wing political party not unlike the others. Faced with the danger of Communist totalitarianism on the Left and Gaullist authoritarianism on the Right, the parties wedded to parliamentary democracy tried to combine in what was called the Third Force. They had a comfortable parliamentary majority over either Communists or Gaullists but they were unable to hold together in any positive policy. The Socialists dared not support measures of an obviously bourgeois color for fear of losing working-class votes. The M.R.P. were too Socialist to get on with the radicals and Right-wing elements and too Catholic to feel at ease with anticlerical Socialists. The main question at issue between the M.R.P. and the Socialists was the old one of State support for the Church schools. The Vichy government had subsidized private — that is, Catholic — schools with public money on which they had now come to depend, and the rise in the French birth-rate during and immediately after the war meant there were more children than could possibly be accommodated in State schools. The State needed the Catholic schools and the Catholic schools needed public money. But the old republican principle was that there should be no religious teaching in the State schools and no State grants for private schools. The quarrel between the M.R.P. and their colleagues on this question did much to weaken the Third Force and to cause the frequent reshuffle of governments in the period after April 1947.

FRENCH FOREIGN POLICY

Throughout all the changes of government foreign policy remained consistent. From 1944 to June 1954 (except for one month) the Ministry of Foreign Affairs remained in the hands of one of two M.R.P. leaders, Georges Bidault and Robert Schuman. The primary problem of French policy was still what it had been since 1870, namely, security against Germany. For this alliances were necessary: first an alliance with Britain (Dunkirk, March 1947), then an alliance with Britain, the Low Countries and Italy (Brussels Treaty, March 1948), then an alliance combining these Powers with the United States, Canada and others (North Atlantic Treaty, April 1949). The two latter treaties were devised primarily for security against Soviet Russia, but in the French view they would serve equally well against any renewed threat from Germany. Yet no one in France imagined that alliances would be enough. Nor could security be attained merely by trying to keep Germany weak: that had been attempted after the First World War, and had failed. In the Second World War Germany had been devastated; she had been deprived of her eastern provinces and was still under military occupation by four victorious powers, including France; but she would assuredly rise again and then, with the industrial arsenal of the Ruhr basin in her hands, she would be much stronger than France.

The innovation in French thinking after 1945 was the realization that opposition to Germany was not enough. What was necessary was partnership, and partnership in a form that would prevent Germany from ever becoming the dominant element. The movement of French thought was toward a United Europe, or at least a federation of the democratic European states. The foundation of the Council of Europe in Strasbourg was intended by the French to be a step in this direction. The Schuman Plan which turned into the Coal-and-Steel Community was an example of the form of partnership which the French had in mind; apart from other advantages it would prevent the Germans from using their coal and steel as a menace to their neighbors. An even better example was the Pleven Plan to Europeanize the Germany army.

Britain's refusal to join the Coal-and-Steel Community or the E.D.C. or to consider any form of federation robbed the French of much of their enthusiasm for these plans; partnership with Germany in which Britain was not a member might leave France at Germany's mercy. There was increasing support in France for the old policy of keeping Germany weak, particularly for depriving her of the industrial resources of the Saar basin. The Saarlanders were Germans and the Saar had been part of Germany before 1919 and again after the plebiscite of 1935, but between those dates the French had ruled the country and after 1945 they were determined to prevent its reunion with Germany. Under French aegis a Saar government was set up under a constitution accepted by plebiscite, a constitution giving the Saar political autonomy but leaving its defense and foreign relations in French hands. A customs and currency union between France and the Saar was signed in 1947 and in 1950 the Saar mines were put for fifty years under a joint board in which the French government had the casting vote. Germany was deeply dissatisfied with all this, and the Saar remained a bone of contention between the governments in Berlin and Paris throughout the early 1950's. An attempt to bury the bone was made in October 1954, when Dr. Adenauer and Mendès-France signed a statute for the proposed "Europeanization" of the Saar, but in a referendum held on this a year later the Saarlanders rejected it by an overwhelming majority.

French foreign policy was handicapped by imperial complications. At the time of the liberation, the French had found themselves in difficulties in every quarter of their vast empire. The trouble arose partly from the fact that the overseas territories had been cut off from the mother country for over four years — and at a time when they were used to sending over half their exports to France and to drawing from France more than half their imports — and partly to the rise of nationalist movements. These movements were successful in Syria and Lebanon which emerged from the war as sovereign republics, and they were gathering momentum in the French protectorates of North Africa (Morocco and Tunisia — see page 130) and of Indochina (Vietnam, Laos and Cambodia — see pages 173 ff.). France tried to meet the difficulty by drawing up a new constitution for the empire, now renamed the Union Française, in which the five protectorates were invited to become Associated States. But Morocco and Tunisia refused to associate themselves and in Indochina a war developed which taxed French military resources to the utmost.

INDUSTRY IN FRANCE

Although neither political reconstruction at home nor French policy abroad could be said to have been successful in the postwar decade, the recovery of France was from other points of view remarkable. It is most easily measured in industrial production. Whereas at the liberation French industrial production was only half that of 1938, by 1953 it had surpassed the 1938 level by 50 per cent. Coal output was then ten million tons higher; steel production had increased by 75 per cent; the production of electric energy had doubled. If the building program for houses, schools and hospitals was in arrears, if wages and prices continued to rise in an inflationary spiral, if many of the nationalized industries were running at a loss and the increase in industrial production was due to a large extent to the finances poured in from the United States under the Marshall Plan, the French could at least feel proud of the re-equipment and modernization of their basic industries under the Monnet Plan and of the recovery shown by the production statistics.

Recovery from this point of view would have gone a great deal farther if the French had not continued to hold to what Anglo-Saxons might call "the French way of life," the life of a man who prefers to be his own master. France was still a country of "small men." Half the total of one million industrial establishments in 1953 still employed no wage earners. No wage earner was employed in 700,000 out of the million and more commercial undertakings. There were two and a half million farms in France, more than half of them worked by one or two persons and only 8 per cent of them employing more than five laborers. This persistence in a traditional way of life may have been uneconomic, and it annoyed the Americans, who especially after 1947 were anxious to build France into the European bastion against Russia, but it made for a continuity, giving France an underlying strength which was anything but apparent on the stormy surface of party politics.

It was from the point of view of world competition that

France's economic recovery was insufficient. Production in the United States, Britain and West Germany was increasing much more rapidly than in France. What was needed, as Mendès-France stated when he became Prime Minister in June 1954, was a structural reform in French economy. His was a remarkable period of office in that he openly set himself to attain four objectives of immediate importance and strained unreservedly to attain them. The first was this "structural reform"; the second was to find a solution to the question of France's relation to a rearmed western Germany; the third was to "reopen the dialogue" between the French government and the peoples of Tunisia and Morocco; and the fourth was to secure a truce in Indochina. This fourth he achieved in one month as he had promised, but he was not given time to reach the other objectives. In January 1955 he was forced to resign after a defeat in the Assembly. No one had any idea how France should be directed except on the lines he had laid down.

PEACE WITH ITALY

The desire of Britain and the United States for a strong, united and friendly France was never in doubt. With regard to Italy there was no such definite feeling. The British had never been able to make up their minds whether to treat Italy as a friend or as a foe. During the First World War she was an ally, but the treatment meted out to her in the peace settlement was hardly friendly. During the period of Fascist dictatorship which began in 1922, Britain's attitude was ambivalent, neither hostile enough to restrain Mussolini from a war of aggression in Ethiopia nor friendly enough to dissuade him from an alliance with Hitler. When Mussolini brought Italy into the war on Germany's side on June 10, 1940, in time to overrun part of the stricken body of France and to launch unprovoked invasions of Yugoslavia and Greece, Britain was able to convince herself that Italy was an enemy. But when the Italians overthrew Mussolini and the whole Fascist regime in July 1943, the British did not know how to take the news. Forty-five days were lost before terms were offered to Marshal Badoglio — forty-five days during which the Germans rushed troops to Italy to meet the invasion of the mainland which the British and Americans had been preparing before Mussolini's downfall. The terms were that Italy should be not exactly an ally but a "co-belligerent." Churchill promised her favorable consideration in the peace settlement if Italians should have "worked their passage."

The Italian campaign proved longer and more destructive than anyone had foreseen. When at last it was over, Churchill and Alexander admitted that the Italians had helped the Allies valuably, not only by action in the resistance movement in the north but by fighting under allied command in the south and by naval cooperation in the Mediterranean. After liberation they continued to work their passage by converting Italy into a parliamentary republic. A referendum of June 2, 1946, showed a majority against the monarchy which had served Mussolini so well, and a general election of the same date provided the basis for a government responsible to the Chamber of Deputies and the Senate. It was the first free election for twenty years and the first in Italy in which women had had the vote. As in France the three strongest parties turned out to be the progressive Catholics (Christian Democrats), the Socialists and the Communists. The Christian Democrats were by far the strongest, polling 8 million votes to the Socialists' 4.7 million and the Communists' 4.3 million.

The elections were a complete repudiation of Fascism. But again the British had their doubts, and the treaty negotiated between the allies and imposed on Italy in February 1947 was punitive rather than encouraging.

By the treaty Italy was deprived of Venezia Giulia, of which the greater part went to Yugoslavia, while Trieste and its immediate hinterland was to become a Free Territory. Italy was deprived also of all her colonial possessions, not only of Ethiopia which had been conquered under Mussolini but the coastal colonies in Africa and the Mediterranean islands in whose acquisition by pre-Fascist Italy Britain had acquiesced. (Ethiopia was restored to sovereignty; Libya was made an independent state in 1952; Somaliland was to be under Italian trusteeship for ten years, after which her independent statehood was to be recognized; Eritrea was federated with Ethiopia; and the Dodecanese Islands were ceded to Greece.) The Italian army was reduced to 250,000 men, the air force to 25,000 and the navy to 25,000, and all the ships of any importance were to be divided between the victorious powers, including the Soviet Union. In this treaty, the Western Powers were more anxious to placate the Russians than the Italians. Reparations demanded from Italy, besides $125 million for Yugoslavia, $105 million for Greece, $25 million for Ethiopia and $5 million for Albania, included $100,000 million for the Soviet Union, a sum considerably in excess of the cost of repairing any damage that might have been done on Soviet territory by the Italian force sent by Mussolini to help the German invaders.

TRIESTE

If there was one thing in the peace treaty that Italians resented more than another, it was being deprived of Trieste, a city which was Italian in population and sentiment. The treaty decision to make it a Free Territory was a compromise between the views of Yugoslavia, who, with Russian backing, wanted to annex it, and the Western Powers, who saw no reason why it should not remain part of Italy. In fact the decision was not implemented. The treaty laid down that the Free Territory should be under a governor nominated by the Security Council of the United Nations and that pending the assumption of office by the governor, it "was to be administered by the Allied Military Commands within their respective zones." But the Security Council failed to agree on a governor, and "the respective zones" continued under military command.

These zones dated back to May 1945 when the New Zealand Second Division entered Trieste and found Yugoslav Communists in possession. An agreement between the military commanders left the northern part of the territory (Zone A), including the city and dockyards and a population of some 700,000, under Anglo-American administration, and the southern part (Zone B), a larger area but with only 73,500 inhabitants, under the Yugoslavs. The result of prolonging this essentially provisional arrangement was to allow the Yugoslav government to turn Zone B into what was in effect a part of Yugoslavia, while the British Commander in Zone A continued to view his responsibilities as those of a temporary caretaker.

A way out of the deadlock — and incidentally a means of depriving the Communist Party of votes in the forthcoming Italian elections — was sought by the British, United States and French governments in March 1948 when they issued a declaration proposing that the Free Territory be returned to Italian sovereignty. This aroused vehement protests from the Italian Communists, the Soviet government and from all Yugoslavs. Even when Yugoslavia left the Cominform in the following June and came in need of outside support against

Stalinite Communists, there was little modification in Tito's attitude. In 1952 he got as far as offering to accept a Free Territory under joint Yugoslav-Italian administration, but this was rejected by Italy. It was 1954 before agreement was reached. The Free Territory, which had never been free, was partitioned, Zone A becoming part of Italy and Zone B part of Yugoslavia. It had taken nine years to settle the Trieste question.

DE GASPERI

After the breach between the Western Powers and the Soviet Union, Italy was rapidly assimilated into the western community of nations. Though debarred from membership in the United Nations by the Russian veto, she joined most of the UN specialized agencies. She was a foundation member of the Council of Europe and of the Coal-and-Steel Community and — what was most important — of the O.E.E.C. and of NATO. For this, much of the credit is due to De Gasperi, the head of the Christian Democratic Party, who, as Prime Minister from 1946 to 1953, proved himself the greatest of twentieth-century Italian statesmen. Under his leadership Italy was made a parliamentary democracy as well as an integral member of the Western alliance. But nothing that he or any one man could do would make the way of parliamentary democracy run smooth in Italy, which was still in many ways the most divided of European states. There was the division between Fascist and anti-Fascist still rankling, as rankle it must after a whole generation of Fascist dictatorship. There was the division between rich and poor, stretching deep and wide from an ostentatious and arrogant aristocracy at one end of the scale to a largely illiterate peasantry and to a couple of million unemployed at the other. The deepest division of all was that between the regions. Italy had always been a country where loyalties were to a town or, at the widest, to a district; and regionalism was traditionally the greatest enemy of central government. The southern provinces, denuded and neglected by absentee landlords, presented a problem which no Italian government before De Gasperi's had dared to face.

The difficulty of parliamentary rule in Italy, as in France, is that no single and united party has ever emerged from the polls strong enough to command an over-all majority in parliament. The Christian Democrats did emerge from the first postwar elections with eight million votes, but on the Left of them were nearly five million Socialists and over four million Communists, and the Christian Democratic Party itself included members ranging from all but the most reactionary to all but the most radical. De Gasperi was able to keep in power only by reshuffling his cabinet no fewer than eight times. When he resigned after the elections of June 1953 his first two Christian Democrat successors tried to maintain their positions by alliances with parties on the Right, and the third, Scelba — who had made an honored name for himself by building up the first efficient and tolerably incorrupt police force that Italy had ever known — by alliance with Left-wing groups. It was all very precarious, a tightrope walk with the Communists, skillfully led by the old Comintern official, Togliatti, watching from the wings. The Italian Communist Party, with perhaps two and a half million members, was the strongest in the world outside the Russian spheres of influence and China.

What would have happened had it not been for British and American aid does not bear contemplating by any except Communists. Britain set the example and United States followed. Marshall Aid made industrial recovery possible. It also enabled De Gasperi to inaugurate a plan for the agricultural recovery of the chronically distressed areas of the south. The 1950 plan for the south provided for a twelve-year investment program in land reform and reclamation, in afforestation and irrigation, in the building of communications and new villages. It was always at the mercy of Right-wing opposition in parliament and of the impatience of the extreme Left. In the nature of things it could not be expected to bear fruit immediately, but the plan was a bold attempt to face a century-old problem for which there had been no earlier solution except by wholesale emigration.

No one could be satisfied by the recovery of Italy in the postwar decade. All that may be said is that it was better than almost anyone — even any Italian — could have expected. After the First World War there were riots, rebellion and a Fascist revolution in Italy; after the Second there was internal peace and the achievement of a close and profitable alliance with the West. The transition to republicanism and parliamentary democracy was made smoothly if not altogether effectively. It was perhaps the happiest and most creditable decade in Italy's history as a united nation.

CHAPTER 5

RUSSIAN POLICY IN EASTERN EUROPE

THE PART OF EUROPE which came within the Russian sphere of influence as a result of the war consisted of eleven formerly independent states. Three of these — Estonia, Latvia and Lithuania — were annexed outright and turned into constituent republics of the Soviet Union in August 1940, an incorporation which, being based on nothing but a faked election, the United States and British governments refused to recognize either at that time or later when the Russians resumed occupation after the German retreat in 1944. (The United States and Britain did, however, recognize the incorporation into the Soviet Union of the northern part of East Prussia, the eastern provinces of Poland, the Ruthenian province of Czechoslovakia, parts of Rumania, including Bessarabia and northern Bukovina, and parts of Finland, including the province of Karelia.) Eight East European states remained nominally independent though obviously in the Russian sphere of influence: four which counted as having fought against Nazi Germany, namely, Czechoslovakia, Yugoslavia, Albania and Poland, and four which counted as having fought on the side of the Germans, namely, Finland, Hungary,

Rumania and Bulgaria. To this sphere of influence was added, with American and British consent, the Soviet zones of military occupation in Germany and Austria. Altogether the territories incorporated in the Soviet Union included some twenty-four million souls. The eight states which, Finland excepted, came to be known as Russia's satellites had a population of roughly ninety million.

The question facing the Kremlin was what use to make of the huge area and population which the Red Army had either "defeated" or "liberated." The answer must clearly be that they must be used to satisfy Russia's deepest and most immediate needs: machinery and security.

The Soviet needed machinery and the means of making machinery — the know-how, the skilled technicians and the machine tools. If the standard of living of the Soviet peoples was to be raised, Russia must have machinery and have it quickly. Could Russia have laid her hands on the Ruhr and the Rhineland, all might have been well. Again and again Molotov was in negotiation with the Western Powers, asking for some sort of rearrangement which would give Russia a share of authority over the Ruhr, but always the British and Americans refused. Russia was reduced to getting such machinery and engineering products as she could out of the countries within her own sphere.

THE DRIVE FOR MACHINERY

The methods chosen were various. From Finland, for instance, Russia demanded in the armistice agreement of September 1944 the payment of reparations to the value of $300 million at the price levels of 1938. As we have seen, a third of that sum was to be paid in wood products, Finland's usual exports, but another third was to be made up of ships and cables and the remaining third of machinery for which Finland did not have the raw materials, machine tools, gigs, factories or the skilled workers. The Russians sent no armed forces into what remained of Finland after the armistice and did not seriously interfere with the internal politics of the country, which remained a parliamentary democracy with a way of life akin to that of Scandinavia and Britain. The important thing was to get from the Finns machinery which Russia could not yet manufacture in sufficient quantity for herself. Given that machinery, the temptation to overrun Finland and to impose a Communist regime on the Finns could be resisted.

The machinery and other goods specified in the reparations bill were duly given, and in September 1952 the reparations account was closed. But Finland was left with an engineering industry which had been built up solely to satisfy Russian demands. It could not now be scrapped and the skilled workers thrown into unemployment, nor could its products be sold competitively on the world market. Finland had no alternative but to keep the engineering industry going and to sell its products to the Soviet Union at whatever prices the Russians might care to offer.

In the Soviet zone of Germany very different methods were pursued. The Russians were in military occupation and exercised, more or less directly, complete economic control. Under the Potsdam Agreement the reparations claims of the Soviet Union were to be met by removals from their zone, particularly of industrial capital equipment, provided that "payments of reparations should leave enough resources to enable the German people to subsist without external assistance." The Russians took no notice of their promise, especially when it became clear that little would come of their rights under the Potsdam Agreement to reparations from the Western zones

FINLAND

ESTONIA

LATVIA

LITHUANIA

U.S.S.R.

GERMANY

POLAND

CZECHOSLOVAKIA

AUSTRIA

HUNGARY

RUMANIA

YUGOSLAVIA

BULGARIA

ALBANIA

GREECE

Miles

0   100   200   300   400

of Germany (15 per cent of such usable capital equipment as the Western Powers should remove from their zones, in exchange for an equivalent value in food and raw materials, and a further 10 per cent without payment or exchange). The Russians concentrated first on extorting machinery by dismantling. By the end of 1946, according to a *Manchester Guardian* estimate, the capacity of industries in the Russian zone compared with their capacity in 1936 was reduced as follows:

Heavy machinery	55 per cent
Iron forges and smelting	80
Electrical	50
Plywood	100
Rubber goods	80
processing	80

Dismantling lost impetus after 1946 and the Russians concentrated on getting reparations out of current production. By July 1948 they had taken by this means about a third of the total zonal production, the most onerous levies being on the heavy machinery and chemical industries. But reparations by dismantling and out of current production were by no means the end of the Russian levy. Soviet corporations established in Germany accounted in 1947 for perhaps a quarter of the total industrial production of the zone, and Russian trading companies, official or unofficial, manipulated the market so as to catch whatever of immediate need might have fallen through the larger meshes of the net.

In the Soviet zone of Austria the methods used were very similar but the justification for them had to be quite different. Austria was not an enemy: it had not been defeated; it had been "liberated." Russia had no right to take from Austria anything except "German assets." The Western Powers maintained that these consisted of such property, rights and interests as had belonged to Germany or to German Nationals before 1938 or had been fairly acquired since then without compulsion. The Russians insisted that they also included Austrian state property which had been taken over by the German government under Hitler and private enterprises which the owners had given up against their will or which the Germans had developed.

Acting on this ample definition, the Russians proceeded to confiscate equipment and installations worth at a rough estimate $200 million. They took over the Zistersdorf oilfields, set up a Soviet Mineral Oil Administration to manage them, raised production from 846,000 tons in 1946 to 3,200,000 tons in 1952 and sent the greater part of the output eastward, allowing the Austrians to buy less than they needed for home consumption. The industrial companies in the Soviet zone of Austria which had been in German hands were put under the Soviet Administration of German Assets in Austria (U.S.I.A.) and their products exported without payment to the Austrians; U.S.I.A. factories did not even pay the Austrian income tax, corporation tax or purchase tax. One way and another, Austria's total losses to the Russians were roughly equal to her gains through the European Recovery Program in Marshall Aid. Russia's most valuable extractions from Austria were not so much in machinery as in oil; the Zistersdorf oilfields were the richest in Europe, with the possible exception of the Ploesti fields in Rumania.

In the satellite states a great variety of methods of satisfying Russia's need for machinery were pursued, but in relation to those countries the main object of Russia's policy was her security.

PHASES IN SATELLITE CONTROL

There were five major phases in the execution of this security policy. The first was the phase of liberation when the Red Army rid these countries of the Nazi invaders and persecutors. In this the Russians could count on a certain amount of popularity especially because they came not ostensibly to impose their own rule but to establish a national government in each country. The Red Army brought local Communists in its train, nationals of the liberated states who had been expelled by their capitalist oppressors and were now returning to take part in the political life of their homeland. Thus Gomulka came back to Poland, Gottwald to Czechoslovakia, Rajk and Rákosi to Hungary, Ana Pauker to Rumania, Dimitrov to Bulgaria. It was an obvious and unexceptionable thing for the Russians to do, and the only pity from their point of view was that they could not do it in Yugoslavia, which had been liberated before the Red Army's arrival and had its local Communist leader, Tito, already in office, with no thanks to Russia.

The second phase of policy was less obvious. Instead of setting up single-party governments of these local Communists, which was well within Russian capacity, the Russians insisted that each state should be under a coalition government of all the main parties which had not been pro-Nazi. These coalitions were given various names — National Front in Czechoslovakia, Independent People's Front in Hungary, People's Democratic Front in Rumania, Fatherland Front in Hungary, and so on — but they were all of the same pattern, consisting of Communists, Socialists, Liberals and members of the Peasant Party, which tended to be the biggest in these predominantly peasant countries. At first the Popular Front governments had some semblance of being genuine coalitions, and their published programs were widely popular since they included not only radical and long overdue social reforms (especially the redistribution of land) but also political freedom and a foreign policy friendly to the Western Powers as well as to the Soviet Union. Only gradually did the local Communists infiltrate the other parties and the Russians increase the pressure toward conformity.

In the third phase the Russians set about the elimination from power in the East European states of all except the local Communists. The purge was skillfully carried out and the methods varied from case to case. Here it was convenient to discredit a non-Communist for having conspired against the victors — Maniu, the Rumanian Peasant Party leader, was blackened with this charge; there it was possible to provoke a pro-Westerner's resignation by subtly making political activity impossible for him — Mikolajczyk, the Polish Peasant Party leader, was eliminated in this way. Often the non-Communist parties could be left nominally intact while in fact their organization was taken over and their leaders replaced by Communist nominees — the Socialist parties were particularly susceptible to this treatment. The timing of this phase differed according to local conditions, but generally speaking its climax was reached in the autumn of 1947, when Mikolajczyk fled from Poland and when Maniu and Petkov, the Peasant leaders of Rumania and Bulgaria, were put on trial. In Czechoslovakia, the most western of the East European nations and the only one which had achieved a genuine parliamentary democracy in the between-war decades, the third phase was reached later and most suddenly. In February 1948 Gottwald's police staged a coup d'état in Prague, and Czechoslovakia came under Communist rule.

ELIMINATING NATIVE COMMUNISTS

It might have been thought that the local Communist parties headed by their national Communist leaders all over Eastern Europe would have satisfied the Russian need for security. But the men in the Kremlin had enough sense to know what while a Communist out of power may be a good internationalist and sincere in his obedience and subservience to Moscow, a Communist in power is apt to become more nationalist than Stalinist. Even if they had not known this already, by 1948 they had the example of Tito to convince them. In Yugoslavia the first phase of Russian policy had not come about. That country had not been liberated by the Red Army but by the local partisans under Tito's leadership. Tito was a good Stalinite Communist whose whole adult life had been spent in Moscow's service, but the end of the war found him master of Yugoslavia, a country which had little reason to be grateful and no reason to be subservient to Russia. Tito naturally put Yugoslavia first, and although the Communist regime he imposed on that country differed at first but little from pure Stalinite Communism, he refused to accept orders from Moscow when they seemed detrimental to his own nation. When Stalin called him to order he resisted, and his resistance was successful; after 1948 there was no question of Yugoslavia's coming under Russian control. With this example before them, the Russians could obviously ill afford to allow local Communists to remain in power anywhere in Eastern Europe.

Thus the fourth phase of Russian policy was the elimination of local Communists from power in the satellite states. Again the methods and the timing varied from country to country. In Bulgaria the native Communist leader was eliminated apparently by an act of God: Dimitrov died in 1949. In Poland

Gomulka was removed from power in 1949, and in Rumania Ana Pauker was removed in 1952. In Hungary and Czechoslovakia the method was to set one group of local Communists against another and then to put one faction on trial and impose sentences so terrible that the survivor would be cowed into subservience. The Hungarian leader Rajk was sentenced to death in 1949, while Rákosi was left in office if not in power; the Czech leaders Slánsky and Clementis were executed in 1952, and Gottwald remained a figurehead till his death in 1953.

Just as the methods of eliminating native Communists varied, so did the means of substituting Russians in positions of power. In Poland it was done quite openly: Rokossovsky, a Russian Red Army general, was made Poland's Minister of Defense and head of the Polish armed forces. But usually it was done under cover in a way less obviously offensive to national sensibilities. National Communists, often of the second or third rank, were left in office, to give their signatures and support to decisions made by Russians at their elbow.

With this fourth phase Russian control of the political life of the East European countries (except Yugoslavia, which had escaped from the net in 1948) was complete. There was no organized body of public opinion left except the Communist parties, and within those parties no personalities who would oppose Russian direction. In every form of secular society from trade unions to universities, totalitarianism had been carried so far that no criticism of policy, let alone opposition, need be feared.

The Russians might well have felt secure, but they did not. It was their misfortune that in the parts of Europe which they had taken into their hands the people were largely of a class and a religion particularly immune to Communist propaganda. The peasants were the largest class, amounting before the war to 34 per cent of the population in Czechoslovakia, 35 per cent in Hungary, 63 per cent in Poland, 75 per cent in Yugoslavia, 78 per cent in Rumania, 80 per cent in Bulgaria. And the Catholics were the largest religious community in Poland, Czechoslovakia and Hungary, where they included respectively 90 per cent, 77 per cent and 66 per cent of the population.

PEASANTS AND CATHOLICS

If there is one walk of life that makes men more recalcitrant to Communism than any other it is that of the peasant, the man who owns the land he works and is passionately determined to go on owning it and working it with the labor of his family and for that family's sustenance, asking little of government but the title to his land and being naturally resistant to all forms of central control. Communists could win the support of the country people as Lenin did in Russia in 1917, and as the Popular Front governments did in parts of Eastern Europe after 1944, by giving them the land, but that made peasants of them, not Communists. It was 1928 before the Bolsheviks felt strong enough even to initiate a Communist policy on the land of the Soviet Union by collectivizing the peasant farms, and then the policy led to widespread resistance and famine. After 1944 they could not afford to wait so long or to risk such a result in the satellite countries.

The obstacle presented by the large number of Catholics of the Roman Communion was even more serious. No other Church can be so recalcitrant to the State. The Free Churches are ill-organized and ill-disciplined; their very freedom makes them inconsiderable as political opponents. The Orthodox and Lutheran Churches are Erastian, traditionally inclined to accept State control. But the Catholic Church, though it may control the State, will never be controlled by it. A further difficulty from the Russian point of view was the fact of Catholics being under the discipline of the Pope, a Western potentate in a Western country, whose opposition to Communism was paralleled only by Communist opposition to the Holy See.

In the fifth phase of their policy in the satellite states the Russians set themselves to break the peasantry and the Catholic Church. What the Kremlin would like to have done can be seen by their action in Lithuania, the only predominantly Catholic nation to be incorporated in the Soviet Union. There the peasant farms were collectivized and the once landowning peasantry turned into what amounted to a rural proletariat under the orders of Communist Party managers sent down from the towns. There the Catholic seminaries were shut, religious teaching forbidden, the priests exterminated and all contact with the Holy See and the Catholic world outside Lithuania cut. But in the satellite states it was necessary to go much more slowly and warily. Collectivization of the land hardly began before 1949. Indeed the whole tendency during the first five years after the war had to be in the opposite direction, for it was necessary to win the support of the peasants and land laborers by increasing their private holdings. In Poland and Czechoslovakia a whole new peasantry was created by settling families on land expropriated from the Germans; in these countries, together with Hungary, Rumania and Bulgaria, over two million families of landworkers received land.

The most sweeping reform was in Hungary, where a handful of great landowners held between them nearly half of the country's land. Under the Land Acts of 1945 some 642,000 families of dwarf-holders, laborers and estate servants got small farming estates of their own.

It was the most popular reform that had ever taken place

in Hungary. Among other advantages it gave the Communists an opportunity for acting against the head of the Catholic
Church in that country. Cardinal Mindszenty openly opposed the reform on the ground that it would deprive the
Church of land on the rents from which the Catholic schools
and much of its other work depended. The Communists
welcomed the Cardinal's opposition: it made him, and by
extension the Church, unpopular. In December 1948 they
arrested Mindszenty and put him on trial as an example of
an enemy of progress and social justice. It was unfortunate
for them that in other countries the Catholic leaders did not
provide such an opening. In Poland Monsignor Wyszynski,
who succeeded Cardinal Hlond in 1948, walked warily. In
Czechoslovakia Monsignor Beran, who had been in a Nazi
concentration camp and could not be accused of being a reactionary, took strong action against priests who were flirting
with Communism, and the Communist government was not
able to win much success in its attempt to split the Catholics
by setting up what it hoped might be accepted as a national,
autonomous Church in Prague.

Two successes could be claimed by the Russians in their
campaign against the Catholic Church in Eastern Europe.
The first was the secession in 1945 of the Uniate Church in
Rumania — a body hierarchically subordinate to the Pope —
to the Orthodox Church, which was under the control of the
Communist State. The second was the excommunication
of Communists which the Pope proclaimed in July 1949. The
Communists had been careful never to say that it was a crime
to be a Catholic; once the Pope had declared it a sin to be
a Communist, they could win support by pointing to papal
intolerance and to the political subservience of the Holy See
to the anti-Communist Powers.

By 1949 the Communists were strong enough in the satellite states to order a drive for the collectivization of the peasants' land. The movement was disguised — in most countries it was described as an invitation voluntarily to join peasant cooperation — and it varied in tempo. Progress was slowest in Poland and Rumania and most rapid in Bulgaria, where nearly half the arable land (excluding permanent pastures and meadows) was organized in the new collectives by 1952. After that year the Communists had to slow down; food was scarce in all the satellite countries, and they did not dare to drive the food producers too hard against their will.

The fifth phase of Russian policy was therefore far from complete when the first postwar decade ended. Russia still had on her western flank people whose religion and peasant way of life were inimical to Communism. But time, the Moscow leaders felt, was on their side, and meanwhile they could feel satisfied that they had established the most thorough political control. They had gone a long way toward refashioning the East European states for Russia's security and they had made remarkable strides in using them to produce machinery. In the economic plans foisted on the satellite governments and the economic coordination imposed from Moscow the stress was on heavy industry and engineering.

CHAPTER 6

AMERICAN POLICY IN JAPAN

WHILE THE RUSSIANS were given a sphere of influence and a relatively free hand in Eastern Europe, the Americans were given a sphere of influence and an even freer hand in Japan. But the relation of the victors to these utterly different areas was not comparable. The Russians entered the countries of Eastern Europe as liberators pledged to restore their national independence; the Americans went into Japan as conquerors bound by no conditions at all. The Russians were connected to the peoples of Eastern Europe by bonds of neighborhood and history; the Americans had no connection with the Japanese, a people whose mentality they were without means of understanding. The Russians knew what they wanted from Eastern Europe: they wanted machinery and security, and their means were communization. The Americans were not at all sure what they wanted from Japan: they wanted security and their means were democratization, but what first appeared as a need for security against a repetition of Japanese aggression turned, after 1949, to a need to use Japan as a bulwark against aggression by the Great Powers of the West Pacific mainland. American policy in Japan was swayed by outside circumstances to a far greater extent than was Russian policy in Eastern Europe.

From the time of the surrender in August 1945 Japan was in the hands of the Americans. It was they who had conquered Japan and their General MacArthur who was Supreme Commander of the Allied Powers (SCAP). There was an Allied Council in Tokyo, consisting of representatives of the Soviet Union and China as well as of the United States and the British Commonwealth, to keep him aware of Allied views, but its powers were merely advisory; and there was an eleven-power Far Eastern Commission to formulate and review basic policies, but it sat in Washington and the Americans did not let their colleagues' views influence them unduly. There were British and Australian and New Zealand troops alongside the Americans in Japan between 1945 and 1947, but after 1947 the military occupation was almost completely American. In fact Japan was under the control of MacArthur and his successors, subject only to orders from the United States President.

It was a task of shocking difficulty that the Americans had undertaken. The towns of Japan had been shattered, not so much by the atomic bombs which destroyed Hiroshima and Nagasaki as by the high-explosive bombing of the larger cities. The destitution of the urban population could not quickly be relieved, for the nation's economy had been destroyed — not merely by military action, which had reduced the number of spindles in the cotton industry by three-quarters and had wiped out the mercantile fleet, but also by the loss of the colonies on which Japan depended for so much of her fuel and food. There were millions of Japanese soldiers to be brought home to a country where there was little hope of finding employment. And the moral destitution was worse than the physical: the Japanese were dazed and brokenhearted by their defeat.

DEMOCRATIZATION

The Allies — in fact the Americans — set themselves two
immediate tasks: to destroy the old militant empire and to
build up a new democratic state. The first task was carried
out with remarkable efficiency during the first year of occupation. The Japanese forces were disarmed, demobilized and,
with the exception of perhaps 300,000 prisoners of war retained by the Russians, repatriated. A few of the more flagrant
war criminals were brought to trial and a great many men of
known militarist sentiments were removed from public life.
Japan was reduced to her home islands, being stripped, according to the communiqué signed in Cairo in December
1943 by Roosevelt, Churchill and Chiang Kai-shek, of "all
the islands in the Pacific which she has seized and occupied
since the beginning of the first World War in 1914" and of
"all territories that Japan has stolen from the Chinese, such
as Manchuria, Formosa and the Pescadores."

The question arose whether the Emperor should be regarded as part of the old militarist Japan or as an essential part
of the new democratic structure. To Russia, China, Australia
and certain other of the Allies he was a war criminal who
should be purged. The Americans took the opposite view.
General MacArthur insisted on his publicly denying his di-
vinity but respected his personal dignity and kept him in
office, not as absolute monarch or even as head of the State
but as "the symbol of the State and of the unity of the people,
deriving his position from the sovereign will of the people."

This phrase appeared in Article I of the new constitution,
which was passed by the elected Japanese House of Representatives a year after the surrender. It was a perfectly democratic constitution, the authorship of which was clearly American, though there had to be a pretense that it was Japanese.

The Americans were in the absurd position of having to force democracy upon Japan. They advocated freedom of speech and of the press while maintaining a rigorous censorship. They insisted that militarism be eliminated from politics while ruling every aspect of public life through their own Military government. They proclaimed the American way of life as the model of pacific, civilian virtue while exemplifying it by warriors under the dictatorial rule of the Supreme Commander.

There was something more than a little ridiculous in the confidence the Americans showed in their work of democratization in the first years of occupation. Yet they had some genuinely democratic achievements to their credit. The Emperor stepped down from his high throne and moved among his people, who came to feel more affection for him and only a little less respect than they had felt before. The descendant of the Sun Goddess was seen as a gentle little man of scholarly tastes — he was a researcher in marine biology. The Americans had succeeded in making a constitutional monarch out of the almighty and distant Emperor. They also succeeded in emancipating the women of Japan, securing for them legal rights, occupational freedom and the vote.

The new electoral system, too, was an American triumph. The general election of 1947 was the first in Japanese history in which the electors were free to vote without fear of coercion. They were free also to abstain from voting, but 77 per cent of those registered recorded their votes, including 20.6 million women who, never having had the vote in the past, were supposed to be uninterested in politics. The choice of parties before the voters was a wide one, though candidates suspected of militarism by the Americans could not stand and the parties were most of them new and strangely named. The Progressives, later called Democrats, were conservative, and the Liberals even more conservative. The Social Democrats were scarcely socialists and the Co-operative Party was even more moderate. Only the Communists fought under their own colors and in open criticism of SCAP. Whether it was for this reason that they had so little success or because of their propaganda against the person and office of the Emperor, there can be no knowing. The fact remains that they won only five seats.

It would seem surprising to the Americans later that they had ever tolerated the Japanese Communist Party. In the atmosphere of 1945–47 they had no alternative. The principles of democracy and the attempt to make a peace settlement jointly with Soviet Russia alike demanded toleration of the only Japanese party which had consistently opposed imperialism and aggression. Founded in 1923, it had been ruthlessly persecuted by succeeding imperial governments. Only three of its known leaders survived in 1945. Of these two were in jail in Japan and were liberated by the Americans. The third, Nosaka, was in China, where he had spent the war years indoctrinating Japanese prisoners. He had had an interesting career in London, where he had studied at the London School of Economics, in Moscow, where he became an official of the Comintern, and in Yenan, where he gained the friendship of Mao Tse-tung. He returned to Japan with some forty Japanese Communists whom he had trained as labor organizers.

There was no doubt that Japanese labor needed organizing. A trade union law, passed in December 1945 with American approval if not insistence, gave rights of collective bargaining and freedom to strike except where such labor groups as the police were concerned. Trade union membership reached a total of six and a half millions within the next three years, and many of the new unions were under Communist leadership. The Americans were soon regretting their generous labor policy. In February 1947 SCAP had to intervene to prevent a general strike. In the following year an act was passed on MacArthur's direction making strikes by government employees illegal. When the second general election was held in January 1949 the Americans and the Japanese employing class were shocked to see the Communists win upwards of three million votes and thirty-five seats in the House of Representatives.

RESTORING JAPAN'S ECONOMY

The labor troubles were as much a consequence of a change in American policy as of the machinations of the Japanese Communists. Between 1945 and 1947 America's policy was intended to be punitive and curative: demilitarization and democratization were the order of the day. The Americans were thinking in terms of a short occupation period, to be ended by a peace treaty which would leave Japan to her own resources. But by the end of 1947 it was obvious both that Russia would not agree to the sort of treaty the United States wanted and that Japan could not live without continued American subvention on a very large scale. The Americans therefore had to resign themselves to a prolonged occupation and to using their best endeavors to help the Japanese to earn their own living. At the end of 1947 Japan's industrial production was still less than half of that of the prewar years, and her exports were not above a tenth of that level; the United States had to finance a Japanese trade deficit of upwards of $300 million a year to avert starvation and a collapse of the whole economy. The new policy must be to assist Japan to make itself self-supporting — a far cry from the policy laid down in September 1945: "The plight of Japan is the direct outcome of its own behavior, and the Allies will not undertake the burden of repairing the damage." The new policy meant getting the Japanese to work: strikes were forbidden and a forty-eight-hour week was introduced. It also meant restoring the Zaibatsu, the big business groups which had been dissolved at the insistence of SCAP by a law for the Elimination of Excessive Concentration of Economic Power. It meant reforming the currency, abolishing the export subsidies and forcing the Japanese to produce at competitive prices, toward which the first step must be the dismissal of redundant employees. No wonder there were labor troubles. But Japan as a whole gained immeasurably from the new American policy. At last industrial recovery was in sight. By mid-1948 the United States government was admitting what would have been foulest heresy and treachery to its allies a short time earlier, that Japan should be helped to win back its prewar supremacy in industrial production in the Far East.

PEACE TREATY AND REARMAMENT

In 1949 a third phase of American policy began. It was the year of Communist victory in China, which changed the whole American outlook in the West Pacific. Communism was the enemy and Communism now covered not only the Soviet Union and Eastern Europe but the whole of China. Japan stood out, not as the imperial menace it had been until 1945, not as the stricken pensioner and pupil it had been until 1947 and 1948, but as a potential bastion of the Western world in the Far East. Therefore Japan must be rearmed. There must be an immediate treaty — no more waiting for Russian and Chinese agreement — a treaty which would make Japan a free and willing ally of the West.

These aims, desirable in 1949, became imperative after the

Korean War broke out in 1950. They involved a revolution
in policy. Rearmament seemed expressly barred by the Ameri-
can-inspired constitution, Article 9 of which laid down:

Aspiring sincerely to an international peace based on justice
and order, the Japanese people forever renounce war as a sovereign right of the nation and the threat or use of force as a means
of settling international disputes.

In order to accomplish the aim of the preceding paragraph,
land, sea or air forces, as well as other war potential, will never
be maintained.

MacArthur got round this by authorizing the Japanese government in July 1950 to establish a National Police Reserve
of 75,000 men to be trained and equipped by the Americans.
SCAP could not persuade the Japanese to rearm more openly
or more lavishly. Public opinion, as well as the constitution,
was against it: the Japanese could not see how they could
afford rearmament or how, in the light of their past experience, a State could have an army without the army ruling the
State. The Americans had to be content with the National
Police Reserve, which by 1954 was 160,000 strong and armed
with a few tanks and airplanes as well as with mortars and
heavy machine guns.

They were determined, however, that Japan's right to rearm should be written into the peace treaty. The Russians
were equally determined that it should not.. A permanently
disarmed Japan, without foreign protective garrisons or bases,
seemed essential to Russian security. The draft treaty which
was negotiated by Mr. Dulles through 1950 and part of 1951
was refused for different reasons by the Soviet Union, India
and Burma. It was disliked by most of the other Powers,
particularly by Australia and New Zealand, but they signed
it at San Francisco in September 1951. Under its terms Japan

was reduced, as the Potsdam Agreement had intended, to its four main islands, the United States retaining trusteeship of the Bonin and Ryukyu Islands. Reparations were not insisted on: "It is recognized that Japan should pay reparations to the Allied Powers for the damage and suffering caused by it during the war. Nevertheless it is also agreed that the resources of Japan are not presently sufficient if it is to maintain a viable economy, to make complete reparation for all such damage and at the same time meet its other obligations." Rearmament was expressly allowed, Japan being recognized as "a sovereign nation possessing the inherent right of individual and collective self-defense."

On the same day that the treaty was signed, the United States concluded a security pact with Japan, providing for the maintenance of American armed forces in and around Japan for international peace and security and also "at the express request of the Japanese Government, to put down large-scale riots and disturbances in Japan, caused through instigation or intervention by an outside Power or Powers."

The Americans had got what they wanted. Japan could continue to be used for the containment of Communism in the northern Far East. But as Mr. Kenneth Younger said in the House of Commons, the treaty "left most of the basic problems of the Far East still unsolved." It was not a general peace settlement; the Soviet Union did not sign it, neither did either Communist or Nationalist China. It was not altogether popular in Japan: the House of Representatives ratified it by 307 votes to 47, but in a House of 486 members there must have been many abstentions. And it left entirely unsettled the question of the economic future of Japan, which itself concerned so many potential clients and competitors the world over.

TOWARD NATIONAL REVIVAL

Japan's economic position was still perilous after 1952. Internal recovery had led to the import of more raw materials but there was no way of finding an outlet for exports of manufactured goods. When orders connected with the Korean War fell off, Japan was faced with a slump. Naturally enough a cry arose in Japanese business circles as well as Communist circles for trade with China. The United States had handicapped Japan in this by forcing Yoshida into a treaty with Chiang Kai-shek which was an open affront to the Chinese Communist government and by imposing on Japan a list of prohibited "strategic exports" which was much more comprehensive than that accepted by Japan's economic competitors, including Great Britain. Japanese businessmen saw no reason why they should not sell to China the machinery and engineering equipment that she needed, buying in return the coking-coal, iron ore, fertilizers and foodstuffs which would be so much cheaper from China than from America. Indeed it was difficult to see how Japan could have an economic future except in trade with China.

Feeling began to rise against the American connection, which increasingly appeared as a bondage. Yoshida, who had been Prime Minister since 1946, fell in December 1954, largely because of his pro-American policy and because he had failed to get from Washington the benefices which might have made that policy seem worth while. In the elections of February 1955 his Liberal party lost over a third of its seats to the Democratic Party led by Hatoyama, who had been purged by SCAP immediately after the war and had no reason to love the Americans. The next biggest gainers were the Left-wing Socialists, who had separated from the others in October 1951 over the peace treaty and security pact with the United

States: they would accept no treaty which did not include the Soviet Union and Communist China. It was not that Japan was "going Communist" — the Japanese Communist Party got no more than three-quarters of a million votes in the 1955 elections — but that Japan's national spirit was reawakening after the shock of defeat and the long years of American occupation and tutelage.

Part Two

THE NATIONALIST MOVEMENTS

INTRODUCTION

WHILE THE MAJOR preoccupation of Europeans and North Americans during the postwar decade was with the Great Power rivalry, that of the majority of the world's inhabitants was with quite another matter. The backward peoples, as Europeans liked to call them, were concerned with gaining their own independence. For them the history of the postwar decade was their struggle against imperialism of one sort or another. This struggle was no new thing, but the course of the Second World War and the subsequent enfeeblement of the West European imperial powers gave encouragement and opportunity which were to bring it to a climax in most parts of the world after 1945.

When the Second World War broke out, the world was still to a large extent under European and North American domination. Latin America had broken away from the Portuguese and Spanish empires more than a century ago, but its republics were still under more or less colonial economy, producing foodstuffs and raw materials for the markets of the United States and Western Europe and dependent on those imperialist powers (the United States seemed imperialist to

the Latin Americans) for the capital and capital goods necessary for their development. Africa had hardly broken the
bonds of empire at all: the whole continent was under the
flag or the military occupation of one or another of the West
European empires — except for Liberia, which was controlled
by American financial interests, and the Union of South
Africa, which was ruled by the descendants of Dutch and
British settlers. The Middle East was a congeries of colonies,
in fact if not in name: Syria and Lebanon were under French
mandatory rule, Palestine and Trans-Jordan under British,
Egypt's Canal Zone was in British military occupation, Iraq
and Persia depended on oil companies owned and operated
by shareholders and citizens of the imperial powers. Only
Turkey was in any real sense independent. In the Far East,
India and Ceylon and Burma were still part of the British
Empire, all southeastern Asia (except for the Kingdom of
Siam) was divided between the British, French and Dutch
empires, and China — though it had shaken off West Euro-
pean bonds to some extent after 1927 — had become dependent on the European imperial powers again and on the United
States in its long battle against Japan.

Between that situation and the situation ten years later is
a difference so great that the period must stand out as climac-
teric in the history of the world.

The movement against European domination — and from
the point of view of the backward peoples the North Americans count as Europeans — would obviously take different
forms in each country, but everywhere it was characterized by
a double aspiration. The native people strove to get rid of
European control, strove to make themselves independent.
But that was not enough, for freedom might mean starvation
and would certainly not mean any raising of the standard of
living. Only by European machines, techniques and methods

could standards be raised. The native peoples must beat off European control with one hand while they beckoned for European assistance with the other. They must assert their own nationalism while welcoming the material culture of Europe. They must insist on their independence from Europe while getting from Europe what alone would make that independence viable.

It would be difficult, but it could be done. Indeed it had been done. Japan in one generation had learned the technique of the West and had beaten Imperial Russia in battle in 1905. Japan had made herself the peer of the European in commerce and industry, while maintaining intact her national religion and civilization. Or, if Japan had made herself a bad example by turning to imperialism on her own account, there was the case of Turkey. The Turks were a backward people in 1919 and oppressed by the Europeans to an unparalleled degree, with the British in Istanbul and the Greeks in Izmir and the allied peacemakers drawing up a treaty to partition the few fertile parts of the barren Anatolian peninsula between themselves — the area round the Bosporus to be an international zone, Izmir and its hinterland to go to Greece, Adalia to be Italian. But the Turks under Kemal had thrown the Europeans out and had asserted their complete independence. Then they had westernized themselves without losing anything integral to Turkish national culture. They had raised capital from the ex-imperialists without putting themselves under dangerous obligations. What the Turks had done after the First World War other backward peoples could surely do after the Second.

CHAPTER 1

LATIN AMERICA

THE SUBCONTINENT OF Latin America was more fortunate
than any other part of the world in the first half of the
twentieth century. Political control by the European powers
had ended (except in the Caribbean islands, British Honduras
and the Guianas) in the previous century, and fear of political
control by the United States was allayed by the good-neighbor
policy of President Franklin D. Roosevelt. Frontier disputes
between the Latin American republics never led to serious
fighting, except in the Chaco War between Bolivia and Paraguay in the 1930's. By the late 1940's the republics seemed
to have solved their problems of international relations. They
had kept out of both world wars, in fact if not on paper. They
had become foundation members of the United Nations, in
which they formed about a third of the total membership,
and played an influential and usually concerted part. And
they had strengthened their ties with the United States and
with each other through the Pan American Union, which at
the Bogotá Conference in 1948 was renamed the Organization of American States.

Two other types of problem, however, were far from being

solved. The first concerned their economic independence. They were fortunate in that after the Second World War there was a huge demand for their natural products — for the oil of Mexico and Venezuela, for the coffee of Colombia and Brazil, for the tin of Bolivia, for the wheat and meat of Argentina. But to continue to depend as they had done in the past on the export sales of these raw materials and food-stuffs meant remaining on a colonial economy and being at the mercy of slumps in the world price levels such as had brought so many of the republics to revolution if not to ruin in the economic crisis of the early 1930's. Somehow they must become more self-sufficient, or at least less dependent on the foreign demand for a single commodity.

The second problem concerned their internal form of government. Although nothing could be more consonant with the rights of man than the protestation of their delegates at meetings of the United Nations and the Pan American Union — or for that matter than the principles inscribed in their Constitutions — the Latin American republics were in most cases governed arbitrarily, in defiance of the rule of law and of the civil liberties. Many of them were still at the mercy of the military *junta*, the plutocratic oligarchy or the demagogue. The postwar decade was as much an age of despots in Latin America as the previous generation had been; it was the decade of Perón in Argentina, Chaves in Paraguay, Odría in Peru, Gómez in Colombia and Trujillo in the Dominican Republic. In the mid-twentieth century only three of twenty republics — Uruguay, Mexico and Cuba — were free from actual or immediately threatened dictatorship. Latin America as a whole was still in a state of political and social ferment. It was still a continent of millionaires and *descamisados*.

But it is dangerous to generalize about Latin America. For all their similarity in history, language and religion, the republics differ profoundly. It may be best to take the postwar story of the four most populous republics severally, the story of Mexico, Colombia, Brazil and Argentina which between them comprise some 111 million of the 155 million people of the subcontinent.

MEXICO

From 1910 to 1940 there was hardly a year when Mexico failed to make headlines in the press of the outside world, hardly a year without a political assassination and never a year without fighting in some quarter of the Republic. It was a generation of revolution, and to the outside world revolution spelled catastrophe. Huerta's rule meant a reign of terror, Carranza's meant corruption and violence, Obregón's regime stood for religious persecution, Cárdenas' for the exploitation of the foreigner. Behind it all the outside world saw Communism, red in tooth and claw.

The Mexican revolution was never Communist; it was nationalist. Its aim was Mexico for the Mexicans, a Mexico national in culture, politics and economics and yet enjoying the freedoms and material benefits of the twentieth century: a Mexico without interference by foreign control, without exploitation by foreign capital, a Mexico without peonage or bondage for agricultural workers on great feudal estates. By 1940 or at least by 1947 the negative aims had been achieved. In the latter year the controversies which had raged for a decade over the expropriation of foreign oil industries were at last settled: United States interests, which had claimed $200 million in compensation, accepted $24 million; British interests, which had claimed $250 million, accepted $81 million in full settlement. Fear of the foreign capitalist had gone, and so had fear of the native landowner. Mexico had become a land of smallholdings and *ejidos*, which are communal or cooperative farming villages with individually worked plots.

Yet the positive side of the revolution remained to be achieved. The Mexicans were still a poor people: rural Mexicans were hardly better off than their ancestors, living in the same shacks, on the same inadequate diet of corn, beans and chili. They were still an illiterate people. The 1940 census showed that 51.6 per cent of the total population could neither read nor write, and the percentage in most areas reached nearly 66. They were still undemocratically ruled in that women had no vote (until 1953), opposition parties had no chance of forming a government and freedom of the press was limited in fact though not in law.

In the quiet years of the Presidencies of Alemán (1946–52) and Ruiz Cortines, the Mexican ruling class turned its whole attention to the positive aims of the revolution. It was a period of "revolution in maturity," symbolized by the change of name of the ruling party from the Party of the Mexican Revolution to the Party of Revolutionary Institutions. By their very nature none of the aims could be achieved quickly. For parliamentary democracy there were no precedents in Mexican history. It was something that at the presidential election of 1952 four candidates presented themselves and all enjoyed comparative freedom of expression and assembly, but it was not surprising that the P.R.I. candidate, Ruiz Cortines, should have received 85 per cent of the record vote. Mexican Presidents are still made by the Party, or rather by the retiring President, who in fact nominates his successor and secures his election through control of the Party; though in fairness it should be recalled that the P.R.I. is widely popular in Mexico and that it is not altogether the President's fault that attempts to form an official party of opposition failed. Literacy, on which parliamentary democracy so largely depends, cannot be made general in a single generation. In a country such as Mexico, with an isolated and heterogeneous rural population speaking a variety of Indian languages, the task of the educationist is heartbreaking. It was something that 3000 new schools, providing for more than a million people, were opened between 1948 and 1950 — something, but lamentably insufficient, for the population in 1950 was nearly a third higher than it had been a decade earlier.

The concentration of Mexican governments in the postwar decades was on industrialization. The war period, when Mexico was largely cut off from foreign supplies of industrial goods, gave an incentive; the years immediately following the war, when Mexican exports sold at boom prices, gave an opportunity. Industrialization was seen to be the means of raising the standard of living of the people and of achieving the economic independence of Mexico. The paradox was, of course, that there could be no industrialization without foreign capital, and that foreign capital might involve a new dependence. But in the conditions of the postwar world and in the maturity of the Mexican revolution, that danger seemed remote. By 1951 the United States Export-Import Bank had contributed $300 million, mostly for public works, and the International Bank for Reconstruction and Development added $34 million in 1949 and $30 million in 1953. By 1954 private United States investors had sunk more than $500 million in Mexico, and U.S. petroleum companies were coming back — subcontracting, for instance, for the Mexican national oil corporation and exploring new oilfields. Most of the new capital went into petroleum, railways and road building, into the production and distribution of electric power, into water and sewage schemes, but always, directly or indirectly, the undertakings were under State control. The government and indeed the country as a whole could look back on a decade of remarkable achievement in industrialization, although the fruits of the postwar investment were in most cases yet to come.

Concentration on industrial development meant a comparative neglect of agriculture. The government had vast schemes for land irrigation and reclamation and could point to a 13 per cent increase in the harvested area between 1948 and 1950, but the condition of Mexican agriculture was still wretched in 1955. There had been too much leeway to make up after generations of erosion, single-crop cultivation and inadequate fertilization. It was all very well for International Harvester to establish their great Saltillo factory in 1948; in 1955 oxen and mules were still the peasants' source of power and most of the plows in use were made of wood. It was a fine thing for Mexico to inaugurate the largest ammonium-sulphate plant in Latin America in 1951; many years would have to pass before the land could have all the fertilizers that it needed. If the aim of the agricultural revolution was self-sufficiency, Mexican progress seemed a long way off the mark in the postwar decade. The most efficiently worked crops were the export crops — sugar cane, tobacco and cotton; the least efficiently worked were corn and wheat, where the yield per acre was only about a quarter of that in the United States. Mexico remained heavily dependent on imported food, especially wheat.

All in all it was a happy decade, successful from the government's point of view, progressive from the people's and most reassuring from that of Mexico's neighbors. Relations between Mexico and the United States, put on a good footing by Roosevelt's good-neighbor policy in the 1930's, continued to improve. Convinced of the United States' sincerity in affirming a policy of non-intervention, Mexican governments in the postwar years led the other Latin American governments in the Pan American Union and rallied to the U.S.

policy of hemispheric collective security. The years of Yankee infiltration and dollar diplomacy were forgotten and commercial connection between the neighbors was happily strengthened. Not only was the United States Mexico's best customer but Mexico ranked next to Canada and Great Britain as the best customer of the United States.

COLOMBIA

The recent history of Colombia has been in complete contrast to that of Mexico. In the half century before 1948 the Republic was calmly and constitutionally ruled by an oligarchy of landowners, reinforced as time went on by men of business. The atmosphere was not unlike that of eighteenth-century Europe, with Bogotá, the capital, earning the title of "the Athens of Latin America" and half a dozen provincial cities having high cultural achievements to their credit. The lay of the land, crossed in the north and west by the Andean ranges, obstructed the communications which were necessary to industrial development and political concentration. Two-thirds of the eleven million people were still making their living from the land, most of them with no tools beyond matchet and matlock and no power beyond that of draught animals to ease their labors. The position of the Catholic Church slowed down any movement for mass education, but if half the children never attended a primary school and the secondary-school children were ill-taught, there were facilities at private schools for the fortunate few. Colombia seemed a sleepy, peaceful country until the upheavals of 1948.

On April 9, when the Pan-American Conference was in session in Bogotá, the Colombian Liberal leader, Gaitán, who was revered as a sage and a hero by the common people, was assassinated. All over the country the people rose, attacking ecclesiastical as well as lay property. In Bogotá, where the mob frenzy reached its height in an orgy of murder, arson and loot, the government did not regain control for three days; the police had taken the side of the mob.

Although the British Ambassador was of the opinion that the rising "bore all the marks of Communist inspiration and direction," it had no leadership and no program and was probably as spontaneous as any rising can be. Gaitán's assassination had set fire to a hayrick which had been smoldering for decades. The Conservative Party had ruled Colombia in conjunction with the bishops on lines which, to put it mildly, were unprogressive. The Liberal Party in the 1930's won control first of the Presidency, then of Congress, and carried through some minor reforms, particularly in the direction of social security, but it was led by rich men largely in the interests of rich men, and in the early 1940's there was a split. At the presidential election of 1946 the Liberals won more votes than the Conservatives but their votes were divided between two candidates, the moderate Turbay and the more extreme Gaitán, and the Presidency went to the Conservative Ospina Pérez. He attempted a coalition government, but by March 1948 it had broken down. Government was in the hands of Ospina Pérez and Laureano Gómez, and the opposition, now that Turbay had died, was led by Gaitán, who seemed certain to be voted into the Presidency at the next election.

The murder of Gaitán and the suppression of the riots which followed put an end to all hopes for social reform. Colombia fell under the dictatorship of Gómez, who had himself been made President as the outcome of a farcical election in 1949 — an election held under martial law, with prohibition of public meetings and censorship of press and radio. By strong-arm methods Gómez succeeded in restoring order.

More than that he could not do. The country needed foreign capital, but conditions were too unstable for investors. It needed alternative exports to that of coffee, but as the postwar years went on Colombia became more dependent on coffee sales than ever. The political situation became more stable after June 1953, when Rojas Pinilla seized power as President. His government acted wisely over the boom in coffee prices in the first half of 1954, taxing coffee exports and devoting the proceeds in part to the building of roads and electrical installations. It checked inflation so successfully that the cost of living rose by no more than 5 per cent between January and August. When the slump began — coffee prices fell by a quarter in August — the government again acted wisely, restricting imports and taxing less essential goods. But Colombia was still at the mercy of the world coffee prices. From coffee came four-fifths of its foreign-exchange earnings. Its economy was still "colonial."

BRAZIL

Brazil borders on Colombia but there is virtually no connection between the two. Their capitals are separated by nearly 3000 miles of territory, much of it unexplored; their people speak different languages and have a different history. What they have in common is the desire to free themselves from the colonial economy. In this Colombia failed in the postwar decade while Brazil came remarkably near to success — so near that, as J. A. Camacho has said, it was "the first tropical colonial area ever to give signs of wholly achieving its emancipation."

In Brazil there was a double need for the drive for industrialization which reached its height in the postwar decade. The first was common to other Latin American countries.

To go on living like an old-fashioned colony would be an absurdity for people of that degree of civilization. A world war might cut it off from its markets. A world slump like that of the early 1930's would always hit the primary producer hardest. There might be good years such as 1949 when Brazil's coffee crop would sell for $500 million, but there would be bad years when it would not sell at all. Brazil must take the course of the United States and any other great infant nation: she must develop her own industries.

The second need rose from conditions peculiar to Brazil. The resources of the country were ample for a population many times as big as Brazil's (which amounted to fifty-two millions in early 1951 and was growing at the rate of a million a year) but they could not be tapped without mechanization on a gigantic scale. The iron-ore deposits represented between a fifth and a quarter of the known deposits of the world, but without transport they were useless. The nuts of the Amazonian forests were said by observers sent by the UN Food and Agricultural Organization to be enough to end the world's food-oil shortage, but they could not be harvested by hand. Two states of the United States of Brazil, Amazonas and Pera, cover an area half as large as that of the U.S.A., but their population is under two million. The opening-up of Brazil was impossible without industrial machinery and twentieth-century technique.

Industrialization would be particularly difficult in Brazil because the country lacked the first essentials, namely fuel and transport. There is little coal, virtually no oil, and hydro-electric energy would need enormous foreign loans; there are few railways, except in the south, and the opening of the vast hinterland by rail transport would cost untold gold. Concentrating their industries in a small area in the south, around Rio de Janeiro and in the state of São Paulo, the Brazilians

made surprisingly rapid progress. By 1949 they were producing nearly all the paper and processing nearly all the foodstuffs needed for their own requirements, and their textile
industry was turning out goods worth nearly £50 million a
year. They had reached a point when they could make most
of their consumer goods. The problem now was to develop
heavy industry, fuel production and transport. A government
plan known as SALTE (from the initial letters of the Portuguese words for health, nutrition, transport and power) undertook to spend £400 million in the period 1950–54, mostly
on rail and road development and hydroelectric plant.

This meant that Brazil must import coal and industrial
machinery and equipment on a large scale. Common sense
should have told the Brazilian leaders that there was no way
of paying for it all except by the export of foodstuffs and raw
materials, which could never be enough to meet the cost of
really rapid expansion, but they thought that they could rely
on foreign loans and tide themselves over by inflation. The
loans — or gifts — from the U.S.A. did not come up to expectation. Loans amounting to $380 million were approved
by the Joint Brazil-U.S.A. Development Commission, but
only $150 million were actually lent before the Commission
closed down in 1953. The $300 million credit given by the
Export-Import Bank to meet Brazil's commercial debt in the
U.S.A. was not enough; Brazil remained crippled by the dollar shortage. There was nowhere for the government to turn
except to inflation. The cost of living doubled between 1952
and 1953, while wages and salaries remained the same. In
June 1954 the minimum legal wage was doubled by presidential decree, which momentarily appeased the workers but
could do nobody any good in the long run. The Brazilian
government had set too fast a pace in the course of industrialization and had brought the country's economy to the
verge of breakdown.

Yet there had been solid achievements in Brazil's drive for heavy industry. There had been, for instance, a development in the São Francisco River at the Paulo Afonso Falls which can be compared only with the United States TVA. A hydro-electric generating plan was set up with a potential of 900,000 kw. to supply the whole northeast corner of Brazil with cheap and abundant electricity. When the Paulo Afonso generators go into full production, a new industrial area will be opened in the northeast to balance the existing concentration round Rio and São Paulo, where two-thirds of Brazil's industrial production was still concentrated in 1954.

The financial crisis of that year brought an end to the career of the most remarkable and long-lived of Brazilian statesmen, Getulio Vargas, who committed suicide on August 24, 1954. In 1945, when he had completed fifteen years in power, he surprisingly announced that he "did not choose to be a candidate" at the presidential elections, and his Minister of War, Dutra, was returned by a large majority. But when the time for the next presidential elections came in 1950, Vargas presented himself again and was elected with a major-ity of one and a half million votes over the runner-up. There was much to be said for his regime. Like other dictators, he had a notable record for draining swamps, for reorganizing the machinery of government in the direction of centraliza-tion and for extending welfare organization. Unlike many others, he carried out a real improvement in education and in health services. Where he failed was in combating corrup-tion in the civil service, in continuing arbitrary rule — muzz-ling the press, imprisoning suspects without adequate trial, dissolving all political parties long after such measures were on any count necessary — and in being overwhelmed by the financial crisis. He was succeeded as President by Café Filho, whose government had no greater success in combating infla-tion. The only way out of the crisis was through more loans from the U.S.A. The Federal Reserve Bank made a credit of $160 million available in September 1954 and a group of U.S. commercial banks advanced $200 million. Economic nationalism had been driven too far in Brazil; toward the end of the postwar decade it was meeting an inevitable check.

One problem has been solved in Brazil more successfully than anywhere else in the world, the problem of racial relations. Brazil has a larger proportion of Negroes than any other independent country except South Africa, yet there is no color bar and virtually no racial discrimination. The descendants of the Negro slaves imported from Africa, of the aboriginal Indians, of the Portuguese colonists, of the Italian, German and Portuguese immigrants have interbred to such a degree that the races are almost inseparable. Brazilians are proud of being white rather than black, but there is no shame in being a Negro. As a member of a UNESCO research team has put it: "People are assigned a place in the social hierarchy depending on their income, occupation, level of education, family connections, and finally, but only of equal importance with these qualifications, on their 'race.' . . . In concrete social situations, other qualities such as wealth, education, family membership, personal attachments and politics seem to determine the way people treat each other rather than 'race.' "

ARGENTINA

The most famous, or notorious, of the postwar attempts to fulfill the Latin American desire for economic independence and political stability was made in Argentina in the name of *Peronismo*. When a group of army officers of which Perón was a member seized power in 1943, Argentina was still a country of rich landowners and poor workers. The workers were already flocking to town and industry was beginning to develop, but government was not adapting itself to the times;

it was still in the hands of professional politicians working for the most part as tools of the landowning oligarchy. Perón was determined to change all that. With all the arts of the demagogue — in which he was seconded if not outpaced until her death in 1952 by his young wife Eva — he appealed to the *descamisados*, the shirtless workers, winning the Presidency in the elections of 1946 and a renewed term of office in those of 1951. With considerable skill and patience he built up a totalitarian police state behind a smoke screen of democratic talk and the façade of a new constitution (1949). He succeeded in breaking the power of the landowners, in keeping the Church out of politics and in holding throughout the postwar decade the support of the working people.

Peronismo had three principal aims: social justice, economic independence and Argentine leadership. The third is the most difficult to take seriously. Perón talked of making Argentina the leading if not the dominating republic in South America, as the United States was in the north, but Argentina had not a third of the population or a tenth of the industrial resources of Brazil. In pursuing the other two, however, Perón revolutionized his country. Social justice meant reducing the wealth of the employers, particularly that of the landowners, and increasing the wealth of the workers, particularly of the workers in Buenos Aires, which with its environs contained four million of Argentina's sixteen million citizens. Perón's labor legislation extended pension funds, sick benefits and holidays-with-pay to nearly all categories of workers, gave employees the right to an annual bonus equal to a month's salary and compensation for dismissal to the extent of a month's salary for every year of service. To the employers all this amounted to some 60 per cent of the direct-wage bill. To the employees it brought no great increase in real wages because of the rising inflation; where the employees gained was in a new sense of importance, in more leisure and in increased family incomes now that women were being employed on an unprecedented scale.

The second aim, economic independence, involved a drive on two fronts. When Perón came to power nearly all Argentina's public services were owned by foreign shareholders. It was necessary to buy these shareholders — most of them American, British and French — out of the Argentine railways, tramways, electric power stations, gas industry, telephone system and water works. But this used up half the country's reserves of foreign currency, which was badly needed for the drive for industrialization. Argentina found itself sadly lacking in capital for re-equipping its agriculture and industry.

Perón's main difficulty was in extending social justice without ruining the country's economy. It was socially just that the workers should have more to eat. To provide them with cheap bread the government bought wheat from the farmers at low prices, and pegged the price of bread. To provide them with cheap meat, exporters were taxed by an ingenious system of differential exchange rates. Perhaps it was socially just to deprive farmers and ranchers, processors and exporters of profits in these ways, but it inevitably led to a fall in production. Wheat harvests sank from the prewar figure of ten million tons to about five million, at a time when home requirements had risen from two and a half to three and a half million tons. Cattle production increased, but the increase in production between 1937 and 1950 was at little more than half the rate of the growth of domestic consumption, and Perón found himself having to insist on two meatless days a week for his people. The same difficulty arose in the industrial field. It was socially just that the workers should have more wages, more leisure, more social services, but if productivity did not at the same time increase, the nation would be no better off.

Perhaps it was to distract attention from the economic situ-

ation that Perón picked a quarrel with the Catholic Church
at the end of 1954. He began to imprison priests for having
tried to suborn the trade unions. He got congress to pass a
bill legalizing divorce. In April 1955 religious teaching in
schools was forbidden, and in May a bill was passed providing
for the disestablishment of the Church. The Vatican replied
by announcing the excommunication of all those who had
been engaged in Church persecution. This was taken as a
signal for insurrection by the navy on June 16. Perón succeeded in putting it down, but in September General Lonardi
led the garrison of Cordoba, the most Catholic of Argentine
cities, in a more widespread revolt, and Perón was forced to
resign the Presidency and to go into exile. General Lonardi's
government was soon felt to be too clerical and too reactionary; he was deposed in November by a group of more
liberal-minded officers.

Europeans and North Americans were inclined to see in
Peronismo merely another form of Fascism, but then they
had seen the Mexican Revolution in its early years as merely
another form of Communism. Latin Americans, whether
favorably disposed or not, regarded *Peronismo* as something
different. After all, it had more social content than other
generals' "revolutions" with which the continent was so sadly
familiar. The appeal to the *descamisados* might be vote-catch-
ing demagogy but it would never be forgotten. The struggle
for economic independence might have cost dear by 1955,
but nobody had expected the accounts to balance after a
single decade of *Peronismo*. Argentine leadership might be
an empty phrase but here was a government which was
frightened of none of the powers-that-be, whether local oli-
garchs, foreign shareholders or the Catholic Church itself.
Peronismo was the same sort of landmark in the postwar history of Latin America as the Mexican Revolution had been
in the history of the between-war years.

CHAPTER 2

THE ARAB WORLD

THE ARAB WORLD stretches from Marrakesh to Muscat, from Aleppo to Khartoum. It has no political or even racial unity; what binds it together is the Arabic language and common membership — in spite of its Christian minorities — of Islam. Its religious focal points are Mecca and Jerusalem, its cultural capital Cairo. The majority of its people are country dwellers (Fellaheen and Bedouin) but a surprisingly large minority are town dwellers, for the Arab countries have a long tradition of city life. Of civilization in the Western, post-industrial revolution sense they have little. Power-driven machinery is a Western innovation of which they are shy; parliamentary democracy is a Western theory and technique with no roots in Islamic society. One day the Arab world will no doubt take big strides toward industrialism and its own form of parliamentary democracy, but in the decade after 1945 it was making only its first tottering steps in those directions. What animated the Arab world in the first postwar decade was the movement for political independence, the birthpangs of a dozen Arab nationalisms.

When the Second World War broke out, the whole of the

Arab world, except Iraq, Saudi Arabia, the Yemen and a few minute sheikdoms on the Persian Gulf, was controlled by one or other of the European Powers. Italy held Libya; Morocco, Algeria, Tunisia, Lebanon and Syria were under France; Britain held the mandate for Palestine and Trans-Jordan and was in military occupation of part of Egypt, with which kingdom she shared condominium over the Sudan. As an outcome of the war, Italy lost Libya, which the victors, particularly Britain, found convenient to recognize as an independent state under its Senusi king. France lost her mandates for Syria and Lebanon, which became independent republics under parliamentary constitutions, soon to be violated by moneyed interests in Lebanon and by military *coups d'état* in Syria. Britain recognized the Hashemite Kingdom of the Jordan which, however, remained dependent on an annual grant of money from Whitehall.

But Egypt and Palestine, the two most sophisticated areas of the Arab world, emerged from the war no farther on their road to freedom. The Western Powers had made Cairo their military headquarters for operations in Africa and the Middle East and had shown disrespect for Egyptian sovereignty to the extent of surrounding the king's palace with tanks until he thought fit to dismiss his ministers and appoint others whom the British believed to be more favorably inclined toward themselves. Under the Anglo-Egyptian Treaty of 1936 the British had the right to maintain a military base in the Suez Canal Zone until 1956, and when the war ended they showed no inclination to reduce their establishment to the limits the treaty prescribed or to prepare for their eventual withdrawal from the zone.

In Palestine the position was more complicated. It was not a simple question of the relations between Palestinian Arabs and British imperialists: there was a third party, the Jews, in occupation of the country, and the Jews were in revolt.

THE JUDO-ARAB WAR

What happened in Palestine after the war was to color the situation in the whole Arabic Middle East. It was the culmination of a state of affairs which had been moving toward crisis throughout the previous decades. When Britain accepted a mandate for Palestine under the League of Nations after the First World War, the undertaking was that there should be — "a National Home for the Jewish people in Palestine . . . it being clearly understood that nothing will be done which may prejudice the civil and religious rights of existing non-Jewish communities in Palestine." Britain's ostensible object was to father the development of an independent state of Jews and Arabs combined. But combined in what proportion? The Arabs felt Palestine to be their own country, and though they had no objection to limited Jewish immigration they regarded any share by the Jews in sovereignty as a violation of the rights which had been promised them in the name of the British government in 1916. The Zionist leaders, whatever their tactical protestations, interpreted a national home in Palestine as meaning Palestine as a Jewish state.

At first, in spite of intransigents on either side, it seemed as though the British object might be achieved. Jewish immigration into Palestine was small during the 1920's, only a few thousand every year. But when the Nazi persecution of Jews in Germany began, the immigration swelled to tens of thousands annually, and soon it was clear that, if the rate were to continue, the Jews would be in a majority in Palestine within a few years. Foreseeing that when the time came for Britain to leave Palestine to ballot-box self-government, it would be self-government by Jews lording it over an Arab minority, the Arabs called on Britain to restrict immigration. Faced with refusal, the Arabs went on strike in 1935 and the strike swelled into a revolt until, in 1939, the British acceded to their demands. That left the Jews with a grievance — and with an example. If the Arabs could get what they wanted by a revolt, so could they. And a revolt by immigrant Jews who had learned something of underground resistance and terrorist methods in their Central European birthplaces would be a much more formidable thing.

The Jewish revolt was conducted by terrorist gangs such as the Irgun Zwai Leumi and the Stern gang, and its first victims were symbols of British imperialism such as Lord Moyne, the British High Commissioner in Egypt, who was murdered in Cairo in November 1944, and British soldiers who were assassinated while on duty in Palestine. The difficulty in suppressing the terrorists was that they had the moral support of the whole Jewish community: no Jew in Palestine would give information against or refuse refuge to a fellow Jew. But it was not this sort of difficulty which prevented the British from crushing the revolt. There were issues of high policy at stake. A large body of public opinion in Britain was in favor of the Jewish cause; the Labour Party, for instance, at a wartime national conference had declared itself in favor of a Jewish state in Palestine. A large body of opinion in the United States was even more vociferously Zionist. The British government was concerned not so much about Arabs and Jews as about its relations with the United States. Britain was no longer strong enough to police the whole Mediterranean and Middle East unaided. France was unable to help, even if she had been willing after the part played by Britain during the war in emancipating Syria and Lebanon from French control and recognizing them as independent republics. There must therefore be American support: somehow the United States must be induced to accept a share of responsibility for the Middle East.

American interest in Zionism gave Britain her opportunity.

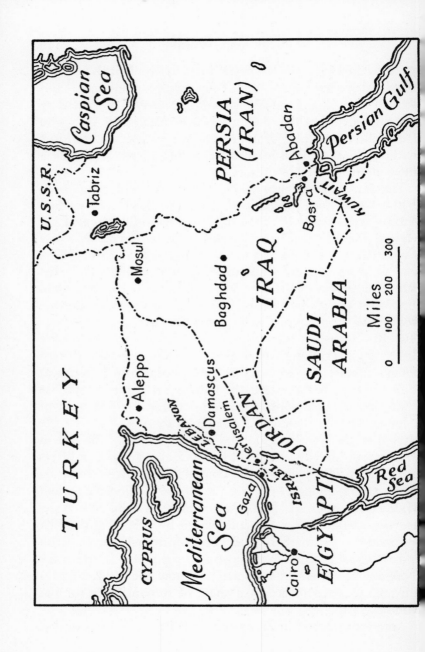

When President Truman impudently proclaimed that Britain ought to admit 100,000 Jews to Palestine at once, the British government proposed a joint Anglo-American commission to report on the whole situation and especially on how such numbers could be settled. If this commission's report were accepted, the United States government could hardly refuse responsibility for its implementation.

The Commission duly reported, but by that time Truman had seen the trap. Britain had to look for another way of implicating the United States in the Middle East. The way chosen was to surrender the British mandate to the United Nations and to withdraw all British troops by May 1948. Withdrawal, it must have been recognized, would be followed by war between Arabs and Jews. War, it was fondly hoped, would oblige the United Nations to act, and that would mean action by the United States.

War did indeed follow, a terrible war which drove half the Arab population out of their homes as refugees to the neighboring Arab states, a war which left the Jews in possession of the larger and less poor part of Palestine, including the New City of Jerusalem and almost all the fertile land. The United Nations took no action. It presided over a first truce signed on June 11, and over a second truce signed on July 18, but when each truce was broken it took no steps against the aggressors. It sent a mediator to Palestine, but when he was murdered by Jews in broad daylight in an open place in Jerusalem, it made no attempt at punishment or reprisals. On the contrary, it recognized Israel, the new Jewish state in Palestine, and welcomed it to United Nations membership.

British policy had failed. The United States had not been drawn into responsibility for the peace of the Arab world (though to the north it had been implicated in the affairs of

Greece and Turkey — see pages 29–30). Morally Britain had the blood of the victims of the Judo-Arab war on her head, for the situation in Palestine had been Britain's responsibility and she had let slip the dogs of war. The outcome was that Britain had no gratitude from Israel, which it had been none of Britain's wish to see born, and Britain had lost the trust and respect of the Arab states. They, it is true, had disgraced themselves in the Judo-Arab war: Iraq and Syria, in spite of much clanking of swords, had taken little effective part in the fighting and Lebanon had taken none; the Egyptian army and air force high commands had proved themselves corrupt; only the tiny Arab Legion of Trans-Jordan, under the training and command of British officers, had conducted itself honorably. Britain was left without a friend in the Arab Middle East, except perhaps Trans-Jordan, now renamed Jordan and including what was left of Palestine to the Arabs.

The Arab states and Israel remained nominally at war. Although there was no formal fighting after the armistice signed between Israel and the various Arab states between February and July 1949, there were constant raids and reprisals across the truce line, which cut Arab hill villages off from their land in the plains and bisected the city of Jerusalem.

ISRAEL

The new Jewish state which had been born in battle developed in the atmosphere of an armed camp. It was surely the strangest nationalist community the world had ever known. All Jews were welcome to its citizenship, and in the first five years of its existence 718,000 new immigrants were received (a number roughly equaling that of the Arabs who had been driven out), including African Jews and primitive desert dwellers from the Yemen as well as sophisticated Jews from

Europe. Of these new immigrants, 47 per cent were from Europe, most of them from the countries under Communist control, 34 per cent from Asia, largely from Iraq, the Yemen, Turkey and Persia, and 15 per cent from North Africa. After 1952 the rate of immigration slowed down and by 1954 more people were leaving Israel than were entering it, but through immigration and natural increase the Jewish population had been more than doubled since May 1948, and by July 1953 it stood at nearly a million and a half.

Tension between new immigrant and old was added to those between religious Jews and irreligious and between townsmen and countrymen. Israel still had to make up its mind whether to be theocratic or a secular state. It had also to decide whether it was to be preponderantly industrial or agricultural. Over 300 new land settlements were founded between May 1945 and September 1953, and it seemed that in future a quarter of the population would be rural. Israel's trade depended largely on this quarter, for half of her exports were citrus products. But Israel's economy depended not so much on her own efforts as on gifts in one form or another from abroad. The deficit in foreign currency in 1953–54 was $145 million. A development plan for the years 1954–60 anticipated the receipt by the government of $1010 million from the United States and from Jewish institutions and $420 million from German reparations. The incongruous bankrupt community was held together by a passion of racial unity and kept alive by a flow of money from Jews overseas — largely from Jews in the United States.

EGYPT

Though the richest and most populous of the Arab states, Egypt after 1945 was in no condition to set an example. The money was in the hands of the pashas, whose lack of social conscience was a world-wide scandal. The power was in the hands of two factions, the Palace and the Wafd, each of them corrupt. King Farouk and his advisers did little but feather their unsavory nests, and the morals of the palace had spread to the Wafd, the once pure nationalist party which the great leader Zaghlul had founded during the First World War to achieve Egypt's independence. Each faction was ostensibly nationalist, as indeed it had to be, for Egyptian public opinion, which could suffer in silence the oppression of the poor by the rich, still had its pride, and its pride took the form of demanding the removal of the British from the Canal Zone and the Sudan.

Suddenly, to the surprise of the Egyptian public no less than to that of the outside world, both factions were overthrown by a *coup d'état*. A group of comparatively junior army officers, with Colonels Naguib and Nasser at their head and the armed forces behind them, seized power in July 1952. They had been humiliated and outraged, as all decent citizens must have been, by the abominable corruption in high military and political circles exposed by Egypt's disgrace in the Judo-Arab war. They had determined to purify the government of Egypt, to reform the economic and social system and to rid the country of foreign control. And they had vowed to do all this without bloodshed.

The remarkable thing is the degree to which they succeeded. Without bloodshed, they got rid of the king and all the wretched palace entourage of panders, intriguers and highly paid advisers. Without bloodshed, they dissolved the political parties. They took power for themselves but used it modestly — each member of the group went on living at approximately his former standard.

To purify the government was obviously less difficult than

to reform the social and economic system. "The social system," as Doreen Warriner wrote in 1948, "is sometimes described as feudal, but it has in fact none of the merits of feudalism, for there is no element of responsibility on the part of the landowning class." The Naguib-Nasser group announced a land reform, a thing which no political party had got so far as even proposing, though there was crying need for it among the two million landowners holding less than an acre each and among the one and a half million casual laborers who held no land at all. The reform announced by Naguib and his young colleagues was small in itself but revolutionary as a precedent. One-tenth of the cultivated land would be taken from large landowners and redistributed in the course of five years: no more and no less. These large landowners would be left with a maximum holding of 300 acres — a great deal in the fertile Nile Valley — and would be indemnified for what they lost at the values they themselves had set upon the land in their tax returns.

To rid Egypt of foreign control, direct or indirect, seemed most difficult of all. The presence of the British in the Sudan and the Canal Zone could appear to Egyptian public opinion as nothing but a threat, but how could the British be persuaded to go without inflaming public opinion to a point where blood must be shed?

In the Sudan the question was what was to replace the Anglo-Egyptian Agreement of 1899, which had established condominium. The Royal Egyptian government had denounced the Agreement in 1951, insisting that it be replaced by Egyptian sovereignty over the Sudan. After long negotiation Colonel Naguib gave way on this point but gained the rest of his demands from the British, who joined him in approving a self-government statute for the Sudan in February 1953. Under the statute, elections were held in November, resulting in a victory for the pro-Egyptian National Unionist Party, and a Sudanese administration was set up in Khartoum as a provisional government holding the reins until after the election of a constituent assembly three years later, when the Anglo-Egyptian condominium would come to an end. Then the Sudanese would have to decide whether the Sudan was to be completely independent or in some degree of union with Egypt. Britain could look back with pride on her record in the Sudan; if it had been an example of imperialism, it was imperialism at its most enlightened and disinterested. The future would be a test for the Egyptians, who would have to learn that the Sudanese might be led but could not be driven, as well as for the Sudanese themselves, left with the problem of applying parliamentary democracy on the British model to a country partly agricultural, partly pastoral, to a people partly Arabic-Islamic, partly pagan and Hamitic or Negroid.

Even longer negotiation was necessary before Egypt won her case over the Canal Zone. Britain had made it into the greatest military base in the world, with workshops, airfields and other fixed installations valued at £300 million and with arms, munitions, spare parts and stores which would cost some £200 million to replace. British propagandists insisted that the Canal Zone was the only possible base in the Middle East and that it was necessary for guarding the waterway which connected the western and eastern halves of the Commonwealth: 60 per cent of all Canal traffic was sailing to or from Commonwealth ports. The Egyptians saw no signs of British readiness to evacuate the zone by the time of the treaty's expiration in 1956. They made it clear by acts of sabotage and terrorism that the British could no longer rely on native labor or on the acquiescence of the Egyptian inhabitants of the zone. At last, after more than eight years of intermittent and often bitter negotiations, the British government gave way.

By an agreement reached in July 1954 with Nasser (Naguib had been dismissed), Britain undertook to evacuate the Canal Zone within twenty months. The base would be maintained by a British civilian firm under contract to the Egyptian government; it might be reopened in the event of an attack on the Arab states or Turkey. This agreement, which was to last for seven years, gave the Egyptian nationalists their hearts' desire. It left Britain with no alternative but to set up a minor base in her colony of Cyprus, where most of the inhabitants were bent upon union with Greece and where the British soon found themselves in the same sort of trouble that they had encountered in the Canal Zone.

PERSIA

Persia (Iran) is no part of the Arab world, but her relation to it is much closer than mere neighborhood. The political, social and economic problems of Persia are very similar to those of the Arab states. The passion of the Persians, like that of the Egyptians, is to rid their country of foreign control, direct or indirect. The revenue of the Persian government, like that of the governments of Iraq, Saudi Arabia, Bahrein and Kuwait, depends on oil which only European and American capitalists can extract, refine and distribute.

What distinguishes Persia's position from that of the Arab states is her neighborhood to Russia. The Soviet government, which showed no serious interest in the affairs of the Arab world during the postwar decade, could not afford to be disinterested in Persia. Its troops had occupied northern Persia in 1941, by agreement with Britain, whose troops occupied the south. An undertaking to withdraw all troops within six months of the end of hostilities against Germany was not kept by the Russians, who remained in occupation until May 1946. They left behind them an autonomist movement in Persian Azerbaijan, but they stood aside and watched it collapse in the autumn of 1945 when the Teheran government resumed control of the province. The Soviet government continued to exercise some pressure on Persia, but by 1949 even that degree of impediment was removed. It was becoming clear that Persian public opinion was turning against the British and that Russian interests were best served by a pose of good-neighborliness.

The feeling against Britain arose from the position of the Anglo-Iranian Oil Company, which had a concession to develop oilfields in southern Persia and had built at Abadan the largest oil refinery in the world. By the end of 1946 the company, in which the British government had a controlling interest, had paid the Persian government £65 million and was providing employment at unprecedentedly high standards for 65,000 Persian citizens. Yet the Persian people as a whole resented the very existence of the company. The oil, after all, was theirs. There was great popularity for the Prime Minister, Dr. Mossadegh, when he denounced the concession to the Anglo-Iranian Oil Company, set up a national oil company in its place and left the British with no alternative but to evacuate Abadan in October 1951.

Mossadegh's was an extraordinary character. To the West he seemed a clown, if not a lunatic. But what seemed absurd antics to the Westerner was seen by the Persians as proof of his warmheartedness and sincere emotion, and what to the Westerner seemed a series of contradictions appeared to the Persians as genuine spontaneity. The Persian character is emotional and a jumble of contradictions; Mossadegh expressed them all, and they loved him for it . His aim was to carry out two revolutions: an external revolution to free Persia from the foreigner, whether British or American or Russian, and an internal revolution to rid Persia of corruption. These essentially were the aims of other twentieth-century autocrats in the Middle East — of Kemal in Turkey and of the Naguib-Nasser junta in Egypt. Mossadegh failed because he tried to carry out both revolutions at the same time. He evicted the British, but that meant losing the revenue on which his government depended and without which no reforms could be financed. His regime was therefore a failure. In August 1953 he was overthrown. The old gang returned to the lucrative jobs in Persia and negotiations were opened for the return of the Anglo-Iranian Oil Company. The settlement reached in August 1954 was that the A.I.O.C.'s place should be taken by a consortium of eight oil companies (in which the A.I.O.C. was to have a 40 per cent share, United States companies 40 per cent, Royal Dutch Shell 14 per cent and the Compagnie Française des Petroles 6 per cent) and that the consortium should pay Persia half of its profits.

IRAQ AND ARABIAN OIL

The closing down of the Abadan refinery meant no loss to Western oil-shareholders as a whole. Had the flow from Persia not been stemmed, there would have been a glut of oil on the world's market. Persian intransigence merely stimulated the development of oilfields elsewhere round the Persian Gulf. Oil production in Iraq had been 4.5 million tons in 1946, in Saudi Arabia 8 million tons, in Bahrein 1 million, in Kuwait 0.8 million. In these countries the concessions were for the most part internationally owned. The Iraq Petroleum Company's shares were held in equal amounts by the Anglo-Iranian, Royal Dutch Shell, an American and a French group; in Saudi Arabia and in Bahrein the concessions were held by American groups; in Kuwait by British and American interests jointly and equally.

Native reaction against the foreign concessionaries was nowhere as acute as it was in Persia. Persia, after all, was an old nation with a glorious history. It would be some time before the Iraqi would equal the Persian in pride or in the belief that he could work his own oilfields. He did, on the other hand, have all the Persian's resentment against foreign control, as the Iraqi Prime Minister, Saleh Jabr, was to realize when the news of the treaty which he signed at Portsmouth with Ernest Bevin in January 1948 reached Baghdad. Under this Portsmouth Treaty Britain relinquished her partial control of the state railways and the port of Basra and handed back the two air bases of Habbaniya and Shu'aiba, though the bases were to be maintained in a state of continual efficiency by the R.A.F. Further, there was to be a Joint Defense Board with equal British and Iraqi representation to coordinate defense policy and Iraq was to be obliged to employ no foreign military instructors except British citizens. The news of this was greeted by riots in Baghdad, in the course of which two hundred people were injured and twenty-two killed. The Portsmouth Treaty was never ratified, and Iraq continued in uneasy recognition of the 1930 treaty with Britain until April 1955, when a new pact was ratified — which was more tender to Iraqi nationalist consciences. The air bases were to belong to Iraq and to be operated by the Royal Iraqi Air Force, though the R.A.F. was to be permitted to station a ground staff on them for joint training purposes.

The Kingdom of Iraq was still dependent on revenue from the Iraq Petroleum Company, but national pride was growing and Iraq was well prepared to lose money in whatever seemed a good national cause. When the state of Israel took possession of part of Palestine in 1948, the Iraqi government

refused to allow the pumping of crude oil to Haifa, a stoppage
which halved its royalties from the I.P.C.

Unlike Persia and Iraq, the other three oil-bearing countries
were hardly states, let alone nations, in the modern sense.
Saudi Arabia was a desert kingdom founded by Ibn-Saud after
the First World War and still under the patriarchal rule of
his family. The state of Bahrein, a group of islands off the
east coast of Saudi Arabia, was still eking out a living by pearl
fishing when its Sheik received his first royalties, a mere
£2200, from the Bahrein Petroleum Company in 1933. In
the sheikdom of Kuwait, a tiny community of fishermen, boat-
builders and traders situated at the head of the Gulf, oil was
not struck till 1938 and during the war the workings were
shut down; but from a production of 0.8 million tons in 1946,
Kuwait's production of oil rose to 43 million tons in 1953.

The effect of oil revenues on these three primitive, patriarchal communities would obviously be revolutionary, though
in what directions could still not be discerned in 1955. All
that could be seen was transformation scenes. In Kuwait, for
instance, where the Sheik's privy purse was swollen by the
direct payment of nearly $159 million in 1953, the flow of
wealth was directed to public utilities and social welfare,
and the little town was transformed in a few years from a
cluster of mud dwellings to a modern city with tarred streets,
car parks, piped water and electric light.

FRENCH NORTH AFRICA

The only parts of the Arab world which remained directly
under an imperialist power throughout the postwar decade
were Algeria, Tunisia and Morocco. Algeria had been in
French possession since 1848. Constitutionally it was part
of metropolitan France, and the statute of September 1947

which pretended to confer a degree of autonomy on Algeria in fact left it as directly under the rule of Paris as before. Tunisia and Morocco were protectorates, France's authority being based legally on treaties with the Bey of Tunisia (1881) and with the Sultan of Morocco (1912), under which French rule was exercised in the name of the local sovereign, without whose signature no law or decree would be valid. The indigenous population was Arab (in Morocco, Arab and Berber) and Moslem, but in each there was a large community of European settlers. It was this settler population which constituted the difficulty. The problem was not simply one of reconciling the strategic and economic needs of the imperialists with the social and autonomist demands of the Arabs; it was also a question of placating the settlers, whose families had developed French North Africa and who regarded themselves rightly as its most valuable citizens and wrongly as its rightful rulers. How much simpler the problem would have been without the settlers can be seen in the Spanish zone of Morocco, where there were virtually none; General Franco's government could let it remain a purely Moslem community and preside over its development toward autonomy, too slowly perhaps for the local nationalists, but very surely.

The nationalist movements in North Africa before 1939 emerged intensified from the world war. France had shown herself impotent in 1940. The British and American forces who landed in French North Africa in 1941 brought talk of freedom: the Atlantic Charter proclaimed "the right of all peoples to choose the form of government under which they will live." Syria and Lebanon achieved their independence; even Libya, whose population was more backward by far than that of French North Africa, became a sovereign state. Egyptian nationalism was in full cry, and there was constant encouragement from Cairo for the nationalist cause in Tunisia and Morocco.

In Tunisia a nationalist party under the name of Destour (meaning Constitution) had been formed in 1930. Its mild demands — responsible self-government under the Bey, and more educational facilities and administrative openings for the Tunisians — were too much for the French. Neo-Destour, a more businesslike party with a more popular backing, appeared in 1934. The French failed to recognize that its leader, Habib Bourguiba, a French-educated Tunisian with an appreciation of French culture and an understanding of what Tunisia had to gain through association with the Western world, was their best bulwark against Moslem extremism in the Protectorate. They dissolved Neo-Destour and arrested Bourguiba in 1938. During the war they went farther: General Giraud deposed the Bey, Sidi Moncef, who in exile in Pau became a national hero and martyr. After the war they found themselves faced with a war-damage bill for 4.5 billion francs and with the effects of successive years of exceptional drought as well as with an inflamed condition of Tunisian nationalism.

The short-lived governments of postwar France were either unable or unwilling to take Tunisian problems seriously. There was an acute shortage of land — the population was multiplying faster than any other country for which there were reliable statistics — but nothing could be done to ease the land-hunger while nearly all the comparatively well-watered area was held by European settlers — by French landowners growing cereals on a large scale and by Italian smallholders engaged in viticulture. No economic problem could be tackled until there had been reforms on the political plane, and these the French were always promising and never carrying out. In 1951 they got as far as to invite three Tunisian nationalists, including Bourguiba, to Paris for an exchange of views, but the outcome was that Bourguiba was arrested again, and the nationalist movement driven underground.

Terrorism increased. It was not till July 1954 that serious steps were taken. Then Mendès-France, the French Prime Minister and Foreign Minister, went to Tunis and asked the Bey to appoint a council of ministers with whom France would negotiate a constitution giving home rule to Tunisia. Representatives of Neo-Destour took part in the ensuing talks, but it was not until June 1955 that a new Franco-Tunisian convention was signed. Tunis was granted home rule under a Tunisian government, while France retained responsibility for defense and diplomatic representation.

In Morocco the French government was equally dilatory and even less effective. The real ruler was not the Sultan, whose powers were only nominal though his prestige was great, nor the government in Paris. Morocco was ruled by the French military and civil servants, with the settlers behind them. A tradition had grown up among Frenchmen in Morocco to ignore orders from Paris. Before and during the First World War Lyautey defied his government again and again, and after the Second General Juin, who was Resident-General from 1947 to 1951, often acted as if he saw himself as a second Lyautey. This insubordination spread down the ranks of the administration until things reached a point at which the French government could not be sure that its most determined policy — if ever it could make up its mind on such a thing — would be carried out.

Serious resistance to the French began in 1944 with the formation of the Istiqlal, or National Independence Party. The French refused it legal recognition, although no one could reasonably doubt that it had the will of the people behind it. First General Juin, then General Guillaume forced denunciations of Istiqlal out of the Sultan, Mohammed V, but that monarch persisted in withdrawing his statement once the duress was removed. In August 1953 the French Resident-General had Mohammed V deposed, using as his tool in this action a mountain chieftain, El Glaoui, the Sheik of Marrakesh. This deposition, of course, settled nothing. It removed the Sultan, whose constitutional position and personal policy might have made a bridge between Moroccan nationalism and a modified form of French imperialism, and it left the French zone of Morocco a prey to terrorism on one hand and military oppression on the other.

The French had to admit their mistake and recall the Sultan. When he returned to Morocco in October 1955, El Glaoui craved his pardon; clearly there had been no genuine opposition to him. On November 6 the French government formally recognized the re-establishment of Mohammed V and declared that Morocco should become a sovereign state, attached to France by ties of interdependence.

Algeria, unlike the Protectorates, enjoyed peace between 1945 and November 1954. Then revolts broke out, spreading until by the end of 1955 there were 5000 Algerian rebels in arms, guerrillas whom the 180,000 soldiers under French command were incapable of suppressing. The nationalist movement could no more be ignored in Algeria than in Tunisia or Morocco. Concessions would have to be made; the only questions were which and when.

It is perhaps surprising that the Arab world, with its bonds of history, language and religion, should have fought its battle in the postwar decade in the cause of separate nationalisms rather than in that of Arabism or of Islam. In the political sphere, if in that alone, there was no unity in the Arab world. An Arab League, including the seven Arab states (Egypt, Iraq,

Syria, Lebanon, Trans-Jordan, Saudi Arabia and the Yemen), was founded in 1945, but it turned out to be more a forum for the expression of Arab rivalries than a focus of unity. Some frail links were forged between Egypt, Saudi Arabia and Lebanon and between Iraq and Trans-Jordan (later Jordan), but the strongest bonds were made outside the League. Iraq made a pact with Turkey and with Pakistan and Persia. To this Baghdad pact Britain adhered in 1955 and with it the United States established military and political liaison, thus to some extent bridging the gap in Middle Eastern defenses against Russia.

In concentrating on national independence each community neglected the social and economic problems which made the Arab world a backward area. Antiquated systems of land tenure and the highest of recorded birthrates led to degrees of poverty unimaginable in Europe. Everywhere the landlords were the predominant influence, and nowhere did the landlords have a social conscience. Enlightened Arabs talked about the nationalist developments of the first postwar decade being a prelude to the social and economic developments of the second. There was little sign in 1955 that this was anything much more than talk.

CHAPTER 3

AFRICA

THE MOVEMENT for national independence, which was in a stage of maturity in Latin America and in adolescence in the Arab world, was only in its infancy in Africa south of the Sahara and the Nile Valley. Economically, socially and culturally, the Africans were still as a whole the most backward people in the world. Politically they were under the rule of Europeans everywhere except in Ethiopia and Liberia, and in those countries African rule provided no model for other parts of the continent: Ethiopia was an autocratic empire, and in Liberia the ruling class of fifteen thousand Americo-Liberians was as foreign to the natives as the European civil servants in the neighboring colonies. Yet by 1945 the ideal of self-government in units exceeding the tribal, if not actually the ideal of national independence, had been conceived in the minds of African intellectuals and was beginning to be recognized by one of the imperial powers.

With regard to colonial dependencies, two changes had been occurring in Britain's policy during the preceding years. The first was that instead of expecting each colony to keep its expenditure within its own revenue, the British government should give money to the colonies to promote their economic development, education and public health. A Colonial Development and Welfare Act of 1940 made £9 million available annually; a further act authorized the spending of £120 million in the 1945–55 decade; a Colonial Development Corporation was set up with powers to borrow up to £40 million from the British Treasury. The second was that instead of regarding only settlements of white men as suitable for graduation from colonial to Dominion status, similar evolution should be encouraged in colored dependencies — in India, for instance, and in the British West Indies, and even, although here progress must necessarily be slower, in certain of the African colonies and protectorates. In Africa this policy involved a transition from Indirect Rule, by which Britain had bolstered up the authority of tribal chiefs, to a degree of parliamentary democracy under which the natives' elected representatives would take over increasing responsibility for the government of multitribal areas. The two changes might seem contradictory but in fact they were interdependent, for there could be no decent self-government for the colonies without financial assistance from outside.

In all this Britain was taking a line widely divergent from that of other imperial powers in Africa. France was also conscious of the need to give money for development and welfare, and established in 1946 a fund (known as F.I.D.E.S.) for the economic and social development of the Overseas Territories, but these territories were regarded as Overseas France, their people sharing in the government of the French Union as a whole through representatives sitting in Paris, rather than as potentially self-governing communities. In concentrating on economic development the French, and the Belgians and the Dutch as well, relied on plantation economy, developing the land, often with great efficiency, through

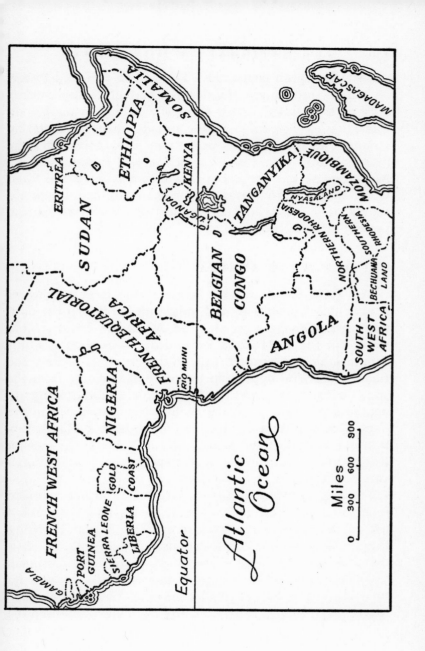

gigantic European companies. The British preferred to rely on peasant economy, restricting the part of capitalist trusts such as the United Africa Company largely to market organization. When Britain made an experiment in plantation economy, as she did with peanuts in Tanganyika after the Second World War, it was exceptional and an arrant failure. More typical was the cocoa-growing industry of the Gold Coast which in 1936 was producing nearly half the world supply of cocoa by the almost unaided efforts of African peasant farmers.

BRITISH WEST AFRICA

The Gold Coast was the scene of the most striking of African developments toward independence during the postwar years. On the map of West Africa the country looks small, but the Gold Coast Dependency is as large as Great Britain itself. The people (4.5 million in 1954) had a tradition of successful opposition to government dating from the 1830's when they forced the British to abandon attempts to impose a poll tax. Their nationalism was germinated in the Fanti Confederation of 1871, in the Aborigines' Rights Protection Society founded in 1897, in the National Congress of British West Africa in the 1920's and in the Youth Conference of the 1930's.

The 1946 constitution for the Gold Coast, which provided for an elected African majority on the Legislative Council but left official members in a clear majority in the Executive Council, was dead before it was born. A new political party, the United Gold Coast Convention, founded by Danquah and Nkrumah, had wide popular support in its demand for full self-government. Disturbances and riots in February-March 1947, leading to 29 dead and 237 injured, induced the

British government to take steps toward a new constitution, steps which were accelerated by Nkrumah's foundation of an extreme nationalist organization, the Convention People's Party. The constitution of 1951 — known as the Coussey Constitution, Sir Henry Coussey being the African judge who had presided over the all-African committee on whose report it was based — gave the Gold Coast a greater degree of independence than any other African colony had so far attained and was clearly intended to lead to Dominion status within a more or less short time. Elections held in February 1951 showed a surprising victory for Nkrumah's C.P.P., which won all but two of the thirty-eight popularly elected seats. Nkrumah became Prime Minister. He led the Cabinet and indeed the people as a whole moderately and well in what was admitted to be a difficult transitional period. In the early 1950's the Gold Coast came to be recognized all over the world as the outstanding example of successful African nationalism.

Developments in Nigeria went parallel to those in the Gold Coast, though lagging somewhat behind. It is the largest colony in the whole British Empire, and its religious, tribal and social structures are so diverse that fusion into a single nation would seem impossible. In the northern region are Moslem Emirates and the people are for the most part settled Hausamen and nomadic Fulani, with Hausa becoming a *lingua franca*. In the south, west of the lower Niger, are the Yoruba kingdoms and east of the river the more democratic Ibos; but interspersed among these three linguistic groups are tribes having little contact with any one of them. In the new constitution which came into operation in 1952, the British government aimed at welding Nigeria into a unity, but it was soon obvious that regional rivalries were too intense for strong central government. The Moslem north showed signs of seceding, as Pakistan had seceded from India (see page 153). It had its own legislature and executive council, and in the Central House of Assembly it was allowed sixty-eight members as against thirty-four for the western and thirty-four for the eastern region, but the Moslems were frightened of the "progressive" influence of other regions. A political party known as the National Council for Nigeria and the Cameroons, founded in 1944 and led by Azikiwe, an Ibo, was demanding a strengthening of central government. The same cry was taken up by Awolowo's Action Group, the party especially of the Yorubas of the western region, which was soon demanding "independence by 1956" for Nigeria, in direct opposition to the wishes of the north. But more than half the total population — 17 million out of 31.5 million — were in the north and there could be no serious question of acting against its wishes either in the degree of centralization or of the timing of independence.

Constitutional changes and debates were not the most important development in the Gold Coast and Nigeria during the postwar decade. Perhaps the most remarkable thing that was happening was the creation of an informed public opinion. Africans were forming not only political parties but youth organizations, women's unions, trade unions and tribal unions, thus disproving the old contention that they were incapable of organizing themselves democratically. They showed a perfervid eagerness for education on British lines; achievements ranged from campaigns against illiteracy by mass instruction to the extension of the University College of the Gold Coast (opened in 1948) and of the University College of Ibadan (1947). The drive for economic development was almost equally striking. One of the first acts of the nationalist government of the Gold Coast was to prepare a development plan on which it was intended to spend £58 million in the years 1951–56. In 1955 industrialization still lay in the future in British West Africa, but it is significant that a mission of the International Bank of Reconstruction and Development reported in 1954 that Nigeria, although "without any industrial tradition, had established a number of modern industries and that Nigerian labour had shown itself fully equal to them."

BRITISH EAST AFRICA

West Africa is a land of Africans. Europeans are few (eight or nine thousand in Nigeria, two or three thousand in the Gold Coast) and hardly any of them would call Africa their home; the only other non-Africans are the Lebanese Christians known as "Syrians," who form a small trading class. In East Africa where a high tableland runs from Kenya through the Rhodesias to the Transvaal, it is different: Europeans live there permanently and regard Africa as their homeland. Thus there is not one potential nationalist movement but two, the black nationalism of the Africans and the white nationalism of the European settlers, to say nothing of the brown nationalism of the Indian immigrants who control most of the retail trade and small-scale industry. The postwar decade was a time of conflict, patent or latent, in all Britain's East African dependencies except two. In Uganda, a country where there were virtually no white settlers, progress was made toward African self-government under the guidance of a liberal governor, Sir Andrew Cohen, whose only mistake was the ill-judged deposition of the Kabaka of the Buganda. In Tanganyika, where the British government ruled conscientiously as a Trustee for the United Nations, there was little racial tension. A new constitution based on the principle of parity between the three races (the population was 18,000 Europeans, 70,000 Asians, 7,500,000 Africans) proved acceptable to the Africans, at any rate as a transitional measure, and some successful experiments were made in encouraging African enterprise, for instance among the Chagga tribe whose Kilimanjaro Native Co-operative Union was a model for coffee-growing on cooperative principles.

Why there should have been so much racial conflict in Kenya when there was so little in Tanganyika may seem difficult to see. It was partly that in Kenya the Europeans were more numerous (50,000) and had acquired a greater part of the best land, partly that they had built a large town, Nairobi, where all the problems of multiracial society were concentrated and dramatized, partly that the British government acted weakly and was inclined to defer to the settlers rather than to insist on its responsibility for the African majority. The white settlers regarded themselves as the rulers of the colony and behaved like a Herrenvolk (some more than others: the British and the immigrants from South Africa tended to be more superb than, for instance, the Greeks). Certainly the white man had brought intertribal peace, banished famine from the land, improved public health, and none but he could have developed the highlands so productively. But there was a natural resentment among the Africans, particularly among the Kikuyu, the largest as well as the most politically conscious of the Kenya tribes, whose rapid growth of population had led to a serious land hunger. A Kikuyu Central Association had been formed as early as 1922 for the recovery of what the tribe regarded as its lost lands. After the Second World War a terrorist organization known as Mau Mau was formed with the intention, it was believed, of driving the white man out of Kenya.

The authorities woke late to the menace of Mau Mau,

and it was September 1952 before a state of emergency was declared and troops brought by air to Kenya. The danger of a widespread rising against the white man was averted, but at the end of 1955 the Mau Mau conspiracy had still not been altogether crushed. By then the terrorists had murdered some thirty Europeans and as many Asians and also thousands of their fellow Kikuyu. Their own casualties were in the region of 8000 killed and 4000 taken wounded in the field, 700 hanged and 70,000 in jail or detention camp. It was the ugliest shock that Britain had had in Africa in the twentieth century.

In Southern Rhodesia settler rule was stronger even than in Kenya and white nationalism had gone farther. The London government's responsibility for the majority (2,000,-000 Africans to 136,000 Europeans in 1951) was less direct, for Britain had granted a sort of semi-Dominion status to Southern Rhodesia in 1923. In Northern Rhodesia, where in 1951 there were only 37,000 Europeans to 1,890,000 Africans, settler-rule was of a different nature: there everything turned on the Copperbelt, and the great opponents of African emancipation were not the owners of the copper mines, some of which were controlled by an American trust, others by a South African company, so much as the European workers who had most to lose by African competition. Their trade union negotiated an agreement with the Chamber of Mines in 1946 by which Africans were effectively barred from employment in any category of job in which Europeans were employed at the time when the agreement was signed. This industrial color bar was unconscionable, but neither the colonial government nor the British government in London dared oppose it for fear of a strike in the mines: the former was dependent on the copper industry for a great part of its revenue and the latter, especially in the years immediately following the war, was anxious for an uninterrupted flow of copper.

A proposal to federate the two Rhodesias and Nyasaland aroused acute controversy. The object was to improve administrative efficiency by coordinating such services as customs and currency, railways and air transport, postal services and electrical supply. Southern Rhodesian settlers pointed out that the only alternative to federation as a means of attracting capital was absorption in the Union of South Africa, and nothing could be worse from the point of view of the African. It was argued by Europeans that the most obvious gainer by federation would be the people of Nyasaland, a fertile, well-watered, crowded district which is the natural granary of central Africa, but which lack of revenue had left undeveloped. If Nyasaland was left to its own financial resources it must continue to be a backward area, living by exporting its young men as unskilled labor to the Rhodesias. Yet the Africans remained obdurate against all proposals of federation because of their land hunger and their fear of an extension of settler-rule. They saw that Europeans had turned the best land in the Shire Highlands of Nyasaland into tea plantations; that they had made Northern Rhodesia depend on revenue from coffee, an undependable commodity as the crisis in the early 1930's had shown; that they had monopolized the Central Highlands of Southern Rhodesia and had concentrated on tobacco growing to such an extent that the country was no longer self-supporting in the most essential foodstuffs. To reply that there would have been no tea, no coffee, no tobacco and no railways or other valuable means of communication if it had not been for the settlers meant nothing to the African. He saw only that there was no longer any room for his family farm.

In spite of African reluctance, the proposal for federation

went through. On August 1, 1953, the Queen signed an Order-in-Council proclaiming the Federal State of Southern Rhodesia, Northern Rhodesia and Nyasaland. The Federal government was made responsible for defense, external, economic and financial affairs, communications and immigration, leaving industrial relations, mining and local affairs to the territorial governments. In the Federal Assembly there were actually to be six Africans among the thirty-five members and three Europeans specially elected to represent African interests. It was not an arrangement about which politically conscious Africans could feel comfortable.

World opinion was puzzled by British policy in Africa. It was hard to understand how the same government in London which was doing so much to encourage and develop African nationalism in West Africa was strengthening settler-rule over the native in Kenya and the Rhodesias and even in Nyasaland, where there were hardly four thousand Europeans among nearly two million Africans. The explanation that settlers' attitudes were changing and that the future would see a new cooperation in multiracial partnership was unconvincing.

SOUTH AFRICA

In the Union of South Africa relations between the races seemed to be moving steadily toward a crisis during the postwar decade. It was the only country on the continent in which, as Colin Legum said, "a European community had achieved its independence from the metropolitan country and established complete domination over the numerically superior African inhabitants." The European community, 2.6 million strong in 1951, was divided into the English-speaking and the Afrikaans-speaking South Africans, the latter descended for the most part from early Dutch settlers, but it was united in its determination to remain dominant over the 10 million non-Europeans. Of these non-Europeans, 8.5 million were Bantu-speaking Africans (known in the Union as natives, though their race's occupation of parts of the country hardly antedates that of the earliest white immigrants), 366,000 Asiatics, most of them Indians resident in Natal, and 1.1 million colored people of mixed race resident largely in the Cape Province.

The postwar years saw the emergence of a peculiar type of nationalism in South Africa. It was not a white nationalism combining Boer and Britain as the great Union leaders Botha, Hertzog and Smuts had tried to do; it was a nationalism of the Afrikaans-speaking white men — the Boers or Afrikaners, who aimed not only at maintaining supremacy over the non-Europeans but at establishing it over the rest of the European population. Their political organization was the National Party, fostered by the three sections of the Dutch Reformed Church and by elements which had been openly pro-Fascist during the Second World War, and led by D. F. Malan until his resignation in November 1954, when he was succeeded by J. G. Strijdom. This party came to power after the elections of May 1948 and stayed with increasing strength for the rest of the postwar decade.

The campaign of the Afrikaner Nationalists against the English-speaking population had not gone far by 1955. It confined itself for the most part to restricting immigration so as to keep down the English-speaking numbers which were already two to every three Afrikaners, and to forays on the language front where they aimed at sending Afrikaans-speaking and English-speaking children to different schools so that they would be taught in their mother tongue and learn the other only as a foreign language. The campaign against the non-Europeans, on the other hand, was pursued unmercifully.

Discrimination against non-Europeans had already gone far when Malan assumed office. The colored people suffered from an economic and social color bar and had the vote only in the Cape Province, where it was subject to educational and property qualifications. The Indians of Natal were not allowed out of that province and were restricted in their rights to own land. The natives — over three-quarters of the total population — were not allowed to own land outside the reserves, which covered at most an eighth of the country, nor were they allowed to rent land unless they lived in the Cape Province and happened to be rich. In Natal and the Transvaal the native might become a labor-tenant, having limited rights of grazing and cultivation in return for his labor and that of his wife and children on the lord's land. If he wanted to migrate to the towns or from one country district to another, he must have a pass. Once he got to town he was debarred from skilled work and forbidden, unless a domestic servant, from living outside the districts scheduled for him. The color bar applied to trains and buses, waiting rooms, swimming pools and public conveniences as well as to hotels, restaurants and cinemas.

Malan professed as his intention the carrying of discrimination to the stage of segregation, or Apartheid. Under his government a Group Areas Residential Act was passed to eliminate existing pockets of non-European settlement in predominantly white areas. A Mixed Marriage and an Immorality Act made criminal offenses of marriage and extramarital sexual relations between white people and those of non-European descent. Early in 1951 he introduced legislation to take the colored voters off the roll in the Cape Province. With all this the opposition parties in parliament, being white men's parties, agreed in general principle. Their opposition was restricted to a desire to make some of the laws less arbitrary and more amenable to appeal to the courts. Serious opposition had to take an extra-parliamentary form. The African Native Congress (founded in 1912) and the South African Indian Congress (1926) combined to launch early in 1952 a "Defiance of Unjust Laws Campaign," in the course of which thousands of passive resisters submitted to arrest and went cheerfully to prison rather than pay their fines. This type of opposition made no impression on Malan, who got a law passed making passive resistance itself a serious crime, and little on the white electorate, which returned his National Party with an increased majority in 1953.

With each succeeding year South Africa drifted farther in the direction of a police state. Yet Apartheid remained a sentimental desire rather than an operable policy, for the white man was dependent on the labor of the non-European majority. Nearly two million natives were living permanently or temporarily in the towns, where the white citizens could not exist comfortably without them. The policy was not so much segregation as intensified discrimination, and the feeling behind it was well expressed by Strijdom when he said: "The white man will only succeed in remaining in South Africa if there is discrimination, in other words, only if we retain all power in our hands."

Britain's embarrassment at all this was extreme. Racial discrimination was contrary to the principles of the Commonwealth of which South Africa was still a member, contrary to the principles which Britain had always professed and was now practicing with such effect in Asia and in parts of colonial Africa. The Union's attitude toward the United Nations was apt to bring the whole Commonwealth into disrepute. It was bad enough when Smuts refused to transfer the mandated territory of South-West Africa to the care of the Trusteeship Council of the United Nations and asked the

UN Assembly's approval for its formal annexation by the Union. It was worse when Malan refused to recognize the authority of the United Nations, declined to submit reports to it and told the Court of International Justice that he would not be bound by its opinion on South-West Africa whatever that opinion might be.

More acute embarrassment arose from the fact that the Afrikaner Nationalists wanted to incorporate in the Union the three territories of Bechuanaland, Swaziland and Basutoland, for which Britain was solely responsible. Malan's case for this was a strong one. The Protectorates of Bechuanaland and Swaziland are adjacent to the Union and Basutoland lies in the heart of it; the tribal boundaries of all three overlap into Union land, and most male Africans leave the territories at some time in their lives for shorter or longer periods of employment in the Union. The South Africa Act passed by the Westminster Parliament in 1909 made provision for the methods of transferring sovereignty to the Union, should that transfer take place. The case against this was that very definite statements were made in parliament in 1909 that there should be no change in the constitutional position of Bechuanaland, Swaziland or Basutoland without consultation with the Parliament of the United Kingdom and with the peoples of the three territories — statements which were repeated again and again in the between-war years. Britain's policy in the territories was to extend the Africans' participation in government and to promote their economic development, for which £2.5 million were set aside for a ten-year plan beginning in 1946. The Africans were clearly opposed to incorporation: in Basutoland, where, incidentally, alienation of land to Europeans was forbidden, a Congress Party was formed to resist Malan's desire, and in the protectorates the tribal leaders were openly opposed to it. So was the British government, though it was sensitive enough to Afrikaner opinion to depose and exile the Bechuanaland chief, Seretse Khama, who had married a white woman.

The position in Africa in the postwar decade was even more fluid than in other parts of the world. Africans all over the continent were developing more rapidly than at any other time in their history. The Europeans were with difficulty either promoting or coming to terms with this development, except in the settler-countries, where attitudes varied from arrant oppression as in the Union to uneasy realization that some new *modus vivendi* would have to be found.

CHAPTER 4

INDIA

Future historians will probably agree that the years immediately following the Second World War were the most dramatic, the most important and, from many points of view, the most glorious in the whole long history of India. The British rulers, *mirabile dictu*, withdrew. In the vast subcontinent with its 430 million people of mixed races and religions — an area which had never been united under one rule before the British came and where democracy was unknown except by British precept — two democratic states came into being, established government according to the rule of law and, so far from fearing or hating their former rulers, chose even in the first fine careless rapture of independence to become members of the British Commonwealth.

Sudden as the British withdrawal seemed at the time, it was in fact the culmination of a process which had been going on for a generation. In the Government of India Act of 1919, Britain fulfilled her promise of "gradual development of self-governing institutions" by allowing Indians in the Councils of the Provinces of British India to control agriculture, education, public health and public works. In the

India Act of 1935 Britain set up the machinery for an All-India Federation to be ruled by Indians except in so far that the British viceroy should have powers in defense and foreign affairs and, in certain special cases, in finance. These steps never went far enough for the Indian nationalists whose party, the Congress, led by such diverse figures as Gandhi, Patel and Nehru, rejected even the offer which Sir Stafford Cripps made on behalf of the British government in 1942, promising an Indian-made constitution when the war should be ended and government by Indians in every sphere except defense. The Congress was determined that Britain should "quit India," totally and immediately.

When the world war ended Britain was ready to quit. The only question was how power was to be transferred to Indian hands in a fashion that would be both orderly and acceptable to Indians as a whole. Britain's intention was to base the transfer on an extension of the 1935 Act, recognizing a sovereign All-India Federation, but now there was a split in the Indian nationalist movement. The Moslem leader Jinnah was demanding a sovereign state of Pakistan which would include the predominantly Moslem areas of the subcontinent. It was becoming increasingly clear that there would not be one independent Indian state but two, and that prodigies of statesmanship would be needed if wholesale war between the religious communities was to be avoided. The British government decided to bring the Indian leaders to a sense of their responsibility by announcing a date for Britain's withdrawal. On February 20, 1947, Attlee declared in the House of Commons that power would be transferred to Indian hands not later than June 1948. If a constitution for the whole of India could not be worked out by that time by a fully representative assembly, Britain would decide to transfer power "whether as a whole to some form of Central Government for British

India, or in some areas to the existing Provincial Governments, or in such other way as may seem more reasonable."

THE PARTITION

Now for the first time leaders of the Congress and the
Moslem League were convinced that Britain was genuinely
determined to quit. They had to turn almost overnight from
rebels against imperialism to rulers. But to rulers of what?
The Congress leaders could never forget their dream of a
united India, but short of a war of extermination against the
Moslems that could not be realized. Reluctantly they accepted the plan of partition put forward by Britain on
June 3, 1947. The British would hand over power to two
states, one calling itself India (unfortunately, because the
word would henceforth be applied with inevitable confusion
both to the whole subcontinent and to the state covering
only part of it), the other Pakistan. The boundary between
them would be difficult to draw, especially in the Punjab and
Bengal, where the religious communities were inextricably
mixed, but detailed provisions were made in the plan for ex-
pressing option and deciding for or against partition in each
province. Britain applied the spur by advancing the date for
the transfer of power to August 15, 1947, and in little more
than two months the whole partition was made. The provinces of Sind, British Baluchistan and the North-West
Frontier Province opted for Pakistan, and the Punjab and
Bengal decided for division. The civil service, army, navy and
air force were divided on a basis of roughly four-fifths to
India and one to Pakistan, a fair enough proportion if we
remember that Pakistan's area and population are about a
fifth the size of India's.

On August 15 the subcontinent became free, free at last

from the British, but no one had reason to rejoice. It was a season of dreadful misery. Communal riots, which had already broken out in the Punjab and Bengal, now spread until millions of people were fleeing from their homes, Moslems to take refuge in Pakistan, Hindus to seek asylum in the new state of India. The number of refugees probably reached six million from each side. How many people died in the exodus or were killed in the riots has never been reliably estimated. The death roll would certainly have been much higher, especially in Calcutta, if Gandhi had not begun a fast which he ended only when the leaders of both communities pledged themselves to communal peace. Nehru was right in saying "I am ashamed of the things my people have done and fear that the consequences may remain with us for a long time." Yet these birthpangs might have been a great deal worse. A population greater than that of Europe was dividing itself into two new and sovereign states; in view of the immensity of the emergency, much more bloodshed and misery might have been expected.

HYDERABAD AND KASHMIR

Apart from the former provinces which were thus partitioned between the two states, there remained some 570 so-called states ruled by princes under British paramountcy. When that paramountcy lapsed on August 15, 1947, the princes nominally had the choice between complete sovereignty and accession to either Pakistan or India. In fact there was no choice for them: all except two were too small and weak for independence, and by the end of August all but those two had acceded. The exceptions were Hyderabad and Kashmir. The former was officially and very properly known as the Nizam's Dominions. The Nizam ruled the area as his

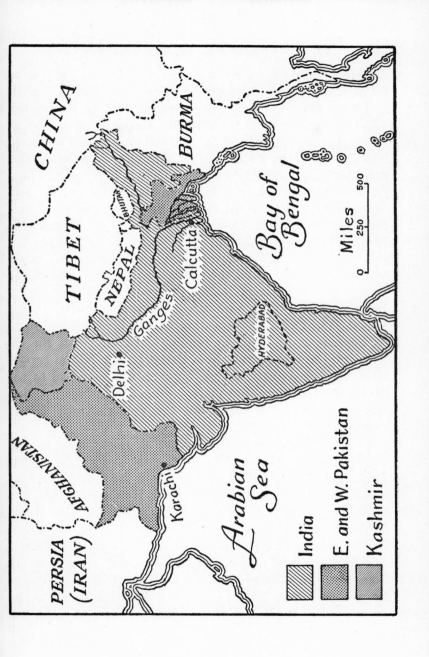

CHINA

TIBET

NEPAL

BHUTAN

BURMA

Bay of Bengal

Miles
0 250 500

Ganges

Calcutta

Delhi

HYDERABAD

Karachi

Arabian Sea

PERSIA (IRAN)

AFGHANISTAN

India

E. and W. Pakistan

Kashmir

ancestors had done for two hundred years and owned it in so far as there was no distinction between his official revenues and his personal income. His desire was to have Hyderabad, which is nearly as large as the United Kingdom, recognized as an independent state, and Sir Stafford Cripps had promised him this when the British should withdraw from India. But now the British would do nothing to help him and he could do little to help himself. His dominions were entirely surrounded by territory ruled from Delhi by the Indian government and he could get no assistance unless by air from his Moslem friends in Pakistan. The Nizam was a Moslem but only two million of his seventeen million subjects were members of Islam; almost all the others were Hindus, who might be expected to welcome democratic government from Delhi. In spite of this the Nizam refused to accede to the Indian Union. The Delhi government replied by blockade and then, on September 13, 1948, by sending detachments of the Indian army to Hyderabad. Four days later the Nizam capitulated. It was regrettable that India should have had to use even a show of force, but incorporation in the Indian Union was surely the only future for the predominantly Hindu "state" of Hyderabad.

The solution in the case of Kashmir might have seemed equally simple. It was a Moslem country under Hindu rulers (3 million of the 4 million inhabitants at the time of the 1941 census were Moslems and only 808,000 Hindus); it might naturally be expected to accede to Pakistan. But the Hindu Maharaja was against this, and so was Nehru, the Prime Minister and undisputed leader of India. Nehru was a Kashmir Brahmin and had a deep sentimental interest in his homeland. In unconsidered moments on political platforms he was promising his followers that Kashmir would be incorporated in India even if incorporation were to mean war with Pakistan. He must have known that Pakistan could never allow that incorporation, for besides the fact that three-quarters of Kashmir's population was Moslem the country was vital to Pakistan in a way in which it could never be to India: its waters run down to the West Punjab and were they to be diverted, as for a few weeks in 1948 they actually were, great areas of the Punjab would return to the desert from which they had been rescued by irrigation.

Fighting actually began in October 1947 with an invasion of Pathan tribesmen from the North-West Frontier, whipped up by religious leaders and inspired by the lust for loot and unhindered, if not demonstrably prompted, by the Pakistan government. The Maharaja fled from Srinagar and wrote to the Indian government offering accession to India and appealing for military assistance. Delhi replied by sending troops which saved Srinagar and cleared the Vale of Kashmir. India and Pakistan were on the verge of open war until the beginning of 1948, when an investigation committee of the UN Security Council, to which India had referred the question, secured a cease-fire agreement and arranged a truce line.

The United Nations mediators went on to try to get an agreement to withdrawal of troops from Kashmir as a preliminary to a plebiscite, but this was always refused by Nehru. As time went on it seemed possible that solution could be found in partition. There were two districts of Kashmir which had a non-Moslem majority and might therefore go to India: Jammu in the south, which was largely Hindu, and Ladakh in the southwest, which was for the most part Buddhist. The northern district which had been the Gilgit Agency was unquestionably Moslem and by 1951 was linked to Pakistan by more than religion and sentiment: there was a motor road from Gilgit to Chilas. No doubt there could have been an agreement over these areas, but there remained the Vale of Kashmir, the most fertile district in the whole subcontinent and one which neither Delhi nor Karachi would see go. By the end of 1955 there had still been no decision. Kashmir was still poisoning the otherwise amicable relations between Pakistan and India.

THE INDIAN UNION

The Constitution of what is officially known as the Union of India was the work of the Constituent Assembly which had been chosen by the provincial assemblies as the result of the elections of 1946. The remarkable thing about it was the way it followed the constitution of 1935, expanding that British-inspired document in directions which the authors had anticipated. The new constitution, which came into force in 1950 and was amended in 1951 and 1953, established India as a parliamentary democratic republic. The old Assembly and Council of State reappeared as the House of the People and the House of States. New things in the constitution were all of British rather than Hindu tendency: suffrage was made universal; princely India was virtually destroyed; the Untouchability of the Scheduled Castes was abolished, at least on paper, and its practice made punishable by law. The last constitutional link with Britain was not severed, for although India became a republic it remained a full member of the Commonwealth and recognized the monarch as "the symbol of the free association of its independent member-nations and, as such, as head of the Commonwealth." Although the official language of the Union was to be Hindi, it was formally laid down that for at least fifteen years after 1950 English should continue to be used for all official purposes, and informally recognized that the English language had created the bond of mental fellowship between Indians in all parts of the peninsula. Relations between the Indian and British governments were friendly and those between Indian and British citizens more cordial than ever they had been before.

The teething troubles of the new state, whose population of 357 million (at the census of 1951) made it the most populous in the world after China, were naturally serious. It was a catastrophe when Gandhi died in January 1948, murdered by a Hindu extremist. Had Nehru not survived and grown from year to year in statesmanly stature no one could have answered for the future of India. Democracy was threatened by Hindu extremists on one hand and by Communists on the other. Fortunately the Congress Party, which had brought the Indian Union to birth, held together to guide it to maturity. At the general elections of 1952, when about half of the total electorate of 176 million went to the polls, the Congress got nearly five times as many votes as the next biggest party, the Socialists, and the Communists polled little more than 5 per cent of the total vote, though with a potentially dangerous concentration of power in the south. Under Nehru's leadership the Indian Union took a position in world politics in some proportion to its strength, adopting a policy of neutralism and standing apart from the Great Power blocs led respectively by the United States and the Soviet Union.

The really serious problems were not political, either in the domestic or international field: they were economic. India was a country of undernourished, disease-ridden people whose expectation of life was hardly more than thirty-two years — in neighboring Ceylon it was fifty-six years. Although seven out of every ten were engaged in agriculture, India was not self-sufficient in food grains. The Indian government drew up a Five-Year Plan, the main aim of which was to attain an annual production of ten million additional tons of food by

1956. A quarter of the total expenditure under the plan was
to be devoted to irrigation, by which it was hoped that some
eight million acres of new land would be brought into use
by river-valley developments and that the yield of another
eight million acres would be greatly increased by the improvement of existing irrigation systems. Another quarter of the
total expenditure was set aside for extending and improving
transport and communications, which would make possible,
inter alia, the processing and distribution of foodstuffs. A
further aim of the plan was to supply the needs of industry.
Provision was made for a substantial increase of cotton growing; half the cotton on which the Indian mills had depended
was now in Pakistan.

No one imagined that the Indians' poverty could be allevi-
ated merely by the spending of public money. The roots of
that poverty lay in ignorance and superstition. While the
population was rising at the present rate — the most moderate
forecast was that India's 357 millions in 1951 would have
reached 410 millions by 1961 — there could be no hope of
growing enough food to fill the hungry stomachs. While
Hindus continued to treat the cow as a sacred animal, India
must be short of meat and dairy products. Nehru did what
he could to encourage the use of Western methods of con-
traception. There was nothing that he, a Brahmin, could
do to change the Hindus' attitude toward cows. The solution
to all these problems lay in long-term education, and perhaps
the most promising of all the Indian government's schemes
was that known as the Community Project, which Nehru
called "the dynamo providing the motive force behind the
Five-Year Plan." It was a scheme to send trained workers to
guide the villagers and to cooperate with them in increasing
agricultural production, improving sanitation standards,
eliminating malaria and establishing schools and adult-educa-

tion classes. According to the plan, some 120,000 villages containing a third of the whole rural population were to be brought under community projects by 1956.

PAKISTAN

The surprising thing about Pakistan is that it should ever have had to come into existence. The proposal that there might be a separate Moslem state was not formally raised until 1940 at a session of the Moslem League at Lahore, and the provinces of which the state should consist were not named until five years later. The Congress was naturally opposed to the whole idea, and so was the British government, which did not countenance the principle of partition until June 1947.

If the birth of Pakistan was a surprise, its survival must seem a miracle. The new state had no history. It was not even a geographical expression, for West and East Pakistan were the best part of a thousand miles away from each other, separated by the Indian Union. There was no racial cohesion to bind the Pakistanis together: the people of the Punjab are Indo-Aryan, descended from the Aryan invaders; the people of Baluchistan and the North-West Frontier are of Turko-Iranian stock; those of Bengal are racially a cross between the Mongol stock of the ancient invaders and the Dravidian aborigines. There was no common language, and the most widespread native languages had no common script. It may be said that English is the language that divides the Pakistanis least, but in English only 1 per cent of the population was literate. The only cohesive principle was religion — nearly 86 per cent were Moslems — but the religious basis was a handicap as well as a necessity, for the religious leaders tended to be socially, politically and economically reactionary and became the main enemies of the government's attempt to modernize the country. Modernization in any case would be difficult enough. Pakistan had virtually no industries: only 26,000 were employed in factories in 1947. The Islamic republic could grow immense quantities of jute and cotton, but the mills for their manufacture were in the Indian Union.

The first eight years of Pakistan's history saw a series of crises any one of which might have been fatal. The first was the paroxysm of partition, during which at least 15,000 people were killed in the Punjab riots and nearly one man in every five in West Pakistan was a refugee. The Kashmir crisis continued throughout those years, sometimes bringing Pakistan and India to the verge of war and always vitiating their relations. A crisis of another nature developed early in 1953 when prices for jute and cotton slumped on the world market and Pakistan seemed faced with ruin. Her great leaders were gone now — Jinnah had died in 1948 and his admirable successor, Liaquat Ali Khan, was assassinated in 1951. The Governor General, Ghulam Mohammed, recalled his Ambassador, Mohammed Ali, from Washington and installed him as Prime Minister in the hope that he would be able to raise help — first in food, then in capital — from the United States.

Mohammed Ali soon found himself involved in a fourth crisis, which had been endemic ever since the birth of Pakistan. Nominally the state was a democratic republic (the decision to adopt the same status as India as a republic within the Commonwealth was taken in November 1953), but the Constituent Assembly had not yet adopted a constitution. The question was whether the country should continue to be ruled by the Governor General with the civil servants and the army behind him or by politicians of the parties which could command a majority in the Assembly. Mohammed Ali took the latter view, at any rate in West Pakistan, and in 1954 rushed through a bill reducing the prerogatives of the Governor General. Ghulam Mohammed replied by suspending parliamentary rule; he established General Iskander Mirza as the strong man of Pakistan, while forcing Mohammed Ali to remain for appearance's sake as Prime Minister.

The overthrow of politician's rule in Karachi was preceded by a similar movement in East Pakistan, which took a rather different course. The crisis was precipitated by the results of the March 1954 elections for 309 seats in the East Bengal Provincial Assembly. The famous Moslem League won no more than 8 seats, while 212 went to the misnamed United Front Party, an incongruous collection including the Communists and headed by a group under Fezal Huq, of whom Jinnah had once said: "He was a curse to the politics of Bengal; he was a curse to Mussalmans because he betrayed us, and a curse to Hindus because he served them as a puppet and their creature." Mohammed Ali lost no time in suspending the constitutionally correct administration of Huq and in putting East Pakistan under the direct rule of the Governor General. In fact it was under the rule of nobody except Iskander Mirza, then appointed governor of the province and its forty-two million people (the population of West Pakistan was only thirty-four million). Between June and September 1954 he did East Pakistan a great deal of good. He banned the Communist Party, which had become a dangerous menace. He convinced the people that they would no longer be either neglected or exploited by the Karachi politicians — and as a member of an old Bengal family he could speak with feeling on this. And he succeeded in getting lavish financial aid from the Central Government for the purchase and distribution of food. But it was all a long way from political democracy.

It would be unforgivable to sneer at this failure of the Pakistanis to put their democratic aspirations into immediate practice. The new state was faced with every sort of difficulty, not the least of which was that there was no precedent for parliamentary democracy in the whole history of Islam. The wonderful thing was that Pakistan survived the first years of its existence without falling either into administrative collapse on one hand or into exorbitant tyranny on the other.

CEYLON

Ceylon's transition to independence was as smooth as that of India and Pakistan was stormy. Britain's intention to "confer on Ceylon fully responsible status within the British Commonwealth of Nations" was never in doubt and there was no difficulty in negotiating the agreements incorporated in the Independence Act of 1947 with the Ceylonese under the undisputed leadership of D. S. Senanayake, the grand old man of the United National Party. Britain got the right to keep a naval base at Trincomalee; Ceylon achieved sovereignty under a democratic constitution. But there was a price to pay for this ease of transition. In India the struggle for independence had been a school of virtue; the older Congress leaders were still in 1955 men who had come to power the hard way and had won their position by personal example. In Ceylon there was virtually no struggle; the United National Party simply found itself in power. While the great Senanayake was alive all was well, but after his death in 1952, Ceylon found itself distressingly short of politicians of stringent virtue.

The infancy of the new Dominion, which did not follow the example of India and Pakistan in declaring itself a republic, was comparatively untroubled. The nearest thing to a crisis occurred in August 1953 when a Communist-dominated trade union brought 7000 Colombo harbor workers out on strike, a strike which soon spread to other unions and turned from passive resistance to violence, leading to twenty-one deaths and the proclamation of a state of emergency. The trouble had arisen from the government's reduction of the rice subsidy, which sent the price of that staple food up by 300 per cent. One could hardly blame the government for reducing the subsidy. Prices for Ceylon's exports, especially tea, rubber and coconut, had come tumbling down; the government had tried to avoid bankruptcy by soaking the rich and only when that had proved insufficient had called on the poor to pay. One might blame the Communist parties for taking advantage of the situation, but one could not be surprised.

It was fortunate for the U.N.P. government that there were at least three Communist Parties in Ceylon, only one of which, under the able leadership of Peter Keuneman, could be called Muscovite. None of them could gain more than ten seats at the 1952 elections, from which the U.N.P. emerged with fifty-four, the strongest opposition party (with eleven seats) being the Independents, a breakaway from the U.N.P. led by Bandaranaike, who was one of the ablest politicians in the island. The U.N.P. had good reason for feeling pleased with itself, although most serious problems lay ahead. One was that of the rapid increase of population: the census of 1952 showed a total of 8.1 millions, an increase of 21.7 per cent since 1946. Another lay in the fact that Ceylon's economy was still that of a colony: the island was still dependent on the sale of foodstuffs and raw materials, and Britain was still its best customer as well as the biggest importer into Ceylon. But those problems could wait. Looking back from the vantage point of early 1956, the outstanding fact was that no other country in South or Southeast Asia enjoyed such peace and prosperity as Ceylon.

The great need of all these countries, if they were to lift their fast-growing populations out of poverty, was capital investment. A conference of the foreign ministers of the Commonwealth, held in Colombo in January 1950, under the chairmanship of Senanayake, led to a plan to meet some of the more urgent economic needs of India, Pakistan, Ceylon and the countries of Southeast Asia. The Colombo Plan inaugurated in July 1951 envisaged the investment of £1868 million during six years. Of this over £1000 million was to come from outside — from the United States, Britain, Australia and New Zealand — and three-quarters of the investment was to be made in India, which included about three-quarters of the population.

From the British point of view the postwar history of India, Pakistan and Ceylon was gratifying in the extreme. Nothing in Britain's conduct in that part of her Empire became her like the leaving of it. Never in history had imperialism left a sweeter aftermath. The adherence of the three newly sovereign states to the Commonwealth was a matter of convenience and self-interest rather than of loyalty of the sort that was felt in the White Dominions, but there was no repudiation of the ideals which the British had lived to inculcate in their imperialist days. "The sceptre may pass away from us," Macaulay had told the House of Commons in 1833, but, "there is an empire exempt from all natural causes of decay . . . the imperishable empire of our arts and our morals, our literature and our laws."

CHAPTER 5

SOUTHEAST ASIA

THE FATE WHICH overcame the white man's empires in Southeast Asia in 1941 and 1942 would have been unimaginable a year earlier. Japan conquered them so easily, rapidly and completely that the awe in which Asiatics had held the white man's power could never be the same again.

The conquest began with the peaceful penetration of French Indochina. France was in German hands and the local French authorities could do nothing but agree to Japanese demands for military bases. The next step was the surprise attack on Pearl Harbor on December 7, 1941, which crippled the United States Fleet. Three days later the British battleship *Prince of Wales* and the battle cruiser *Renown* were sunk in the Gulf of Siam. Japan now had naval and air supremacy. The great British base of Singapore surrendered on February 15, 1942. By March the Japanese had a footing in the Dutch East Indies. Soon there was nothing left to the white man in all Southeast Asia beyond a precarious footing in Burma.

Not in French Indochina nor in the British dependencies of Burma, Malaya and Singapore, nor in the Dutch East

Indies, nor, to any great extent, in the American Philippines did the natives offer serious resistance. For the most part they had not been trained to resist; they had been taught to rely on the white man's protection. But that was not the main reason for their passivity. The Japanese came as a kindred people with the slogan of "Asia for the Asiatics." It was a prospect much more attractive to the peoples of Southeast Asia than any that had been held out by Europeans. The Japanese soon belied their golden promises, but when the time of their surrender came in 1945 they left behind them in many parts of the subcontinent and islands nationalist movements which would make the re-establishment of the white man's empires difficult if not altogether impossible.

The victors were in no state of agreement about Southeast Asia. The Americans were in favor of ending colonialism (they were not to come alive to strategic interests beyond the Philippines until after the victory of the Communists in China in 1949). The British were of two minds: they were prepared to hand Burma over, in their own good time, to the Burmese, but there could be no question of leaving Malaya to the natives (see pages 180 ff.). They were ready to recognize French rights in Indochina and Dutch rights in the East Indies (Indonesia), but not ready to suppress the nationalist movements during the few crucial months before the French and Dutch could collect ships and troops and make their return to Southeast Asia. The outcome was a decade of unparalleled upheaval, from which nationalism in various forms emerged triumphant in Burma, Indochina and Indonesia. Only Siam was immune to the crisis, Siam the one country which had never been reduced to colonial status and where nationalism was satisfied. The Siamese government bowed before the winds, becoming a collaborator of the Japanese, then at the right moment surrendering to the British, and later, when the Cold War came, entering the Western alliance for the containment of Communism.

If the story of Siam was the simplest and smoothest in the Southeast Asia of the postwar decade, that of Burma was the most complicated. To a greater extent than that of any of the other countries, Burma had been a battlefield. When the war ended, most of her inland towns were in ruins and Rangoon itself was at a standstill, its port unusable. Throughout the country the R.A.F. had wrecked railways and bridges. Burma had been deprived of its imports — including clothing, almost all of which was imported — and it must be years before the export industries (rice, teak and oil) could be restored. The Japanese occupation had not united the 17,000,000 people of Burma; it had divided them. The Burmans had on the whole acquiesced in it and so had the Shans at the frontier area, but the other frontier peoples, the Kachins and the Shins and the Karens (who had once been a frontier people but who were now inextricably mixed with the Burmans of the Plains) had resisted and fought bravely alongside the British. A prosperous, united, self-governing Burma seemed too much to hope for.

Britain's policy as defined in a White Paper of May 1945 was to promote in due course self-government for Burma within the British Commonwealth. Before the new constitution could be drawn up by representatives of the Burmese peoples, there was to be a period of direct rule by the British Governor. This was more than nationalists could stand. Some of them had had a taste of office, if not of power, under the Japanese and were in no mood to be demoted by the British. Others had formed a spearhead of revolutionary na-

CHINA

BURMA

INDIA

N. VIETNAM

Hanoi

Hainan

LAOS

Rangoon

SIAM

S. VIETNAM

Bangkok

CAMBODIA

Andaman
Islands

Saigon

Nantoena Is.

MALAYA

Singapore

BORNEO

SUMATRA

Miles

0   100   200   300   400

JAVA

Jakarta

tionalism: a group of young men mostly from the University of Rangoon and led by Aung San had escaped to Japan early in the war and later returned to Burma with the Japanese invaders. They had intended to use the Japanese against the British, but when they found that the Japanese were using them, they broke away, formed the resistance forces into an Anti-Fascist People's Freedom League (A.F.P.F.L.) and got this organization's support accepted by the British in March 1945. They were in no mood to submit to a British governor's rule. They organized strikes and forced the British government to change its policy.

The agreement reached between Aung San and the British government in January 1947 provided for the election of a Constitutional Assembly in Burma which would lead to its independence. It was agreed that "while the British Government hoped that Burma might decide to remain a member of the British Commonwealth, the choice rested completely with the Burmese." Elections followed in April, giving the A.F.P.F.L. 173 out of the 210 seats, and the Assembly resolved to set up an independent republic outside the Commonwealth. There was a setback in July when Aung San and six of his ministerial colleagues were murdered, but his friend Thakin Nu (now called U Nu) succeeded him as Prime Minister and signed in October the treaty with Britain by which Burma was recognized as a sovereign state.

Five great problems faced the new republic. The first was dacoity (armed banditry), which in the first quarter of 1947 had been responsible for 733 murders and 5743 cases of robbery with violence. The second was the armed opposition of the Communists, two rival groups of them, each with an irregular army. The third was the problem of relations between the Burman majority and the frontier peoples and Karens, who had neither culture nor, in many cases, religion in common with the Buddhist Burmans. The new Constitution provided protection and special representation for these racial minorities, but by January 1949 the Karens were up in arms: they cut communications between Rangoon and the north and were fighting in the suburbs of the capital.

To the surprise of the outside world U Nu's government was able to bring these first three problems within sight of solution by the middle of 1950. It was a Left-wing government with a policy of state socialism and the support of the Socialist Party. It stood for Burma for the Burmese, that is for the racial minorities as well as for the Burmans, and for the poor against the rich of any race. Gradually its intentions began to be realized, and its political and military force to be felt. Dacoity diminished, the Communists lost their élan and the Karenni fighters laid down their arms.

The two greatest problems, however, remained. One, common to all newly independent states, was how to create an efficient and trustworthy class to do the professional and administrative work. It was particularly acute in Burma, where the British-built educational system had trained few people beyond clerks and lawyers; in 1936–37, for instance, only two engineers and four doctors had graduated from the University of Rangoon. The other problem was that of restoring the rice, timber and oil industries on which the country depended for its livelihood. The only solution was to attract foreign capital, and to attract it in such a way as not to bring back foreign control or mastery in any form. U Nu played his cards carefully, appealing to foreign governments who had reason to fear the spread of Communism. Subventions reached Burma first through the U.S. Economic Co-operation Administration, then through Britain, Pakistan, India and Ceylon, who made a joint loan of £6 million in March 1951, then through the Colombo Plan.

INDOCHINA

The struggle in the postwar decade involved only part of Indochina. Laos and Cambodia remained on the whole outside the melee, which was confined to the largely Annamese countries of Tonkin, Annam and Cochin China, which together comprise Vietnam. It is a densely populated country, especially in the Red River delta round Hanoi in the north and in the Mekong River delta round Saigon in the south. The French had done a great deal to develop Vietnam, turning it into the third rice-exporting country of Southeast Asia, but overpopulation in the north and landlordism in the south had led to much economic discontent and there was a widespread feeling that Vietnam was being run by the French in the interests of France. A nationalist organization, Vietminh, or the League for the Independence of Vietnam, had been formed in 1939 but few people beyond its leaders took it seriously. Chief among them was a Communist now calling himself Ho Chi Minh (He Who Shines), who had emigrated to Paris as a boy and had spent three years in Moscow in the early 1920's before being sent to China to work under Borodin.

Allied leaders were divided in their opinions on the future of Indochina. Roosevelt was opposed to the return of French colonialism and would have liked to see its occupation by Nationalist China under Chiang Kai-shek. At Potsdam it was decided that Chinese occupation should be temporary and confined to the area north of the 16th parallel of latitude, while the British should occupy the area to the south, pending the return of the French. After the Japanese surrender the Chinese Nationalists cooperated with Ho Chi Minh and made difficulties for the resumption of French authority. The British forces did not arrive until a month after the surrender, when Ho Chi Minh had already been proclaimed President of the Republic of Vietnam; it was all they could do to help French officials to suppress his followers in the south.

In February 1946 the Chinese at last evacuated northern Vietnam, and by this time Ho Chi Minh had consolidated his position. The French government negotiated with him, but the degree of autonomy they offered fell far short of Home Rule, let alone of independence, and the nationalist revolt under Vietminh turned to open war by the end of the year.

The French were determined to suppress the rebels by old-fashioned imperialist methods, and the liberal promises which were made from time to time by Ministers in Paris were belied by French military leaders on the spot. Any chance the French might have had of winning such a war was ended by the triumph of the Communists in China. Ho Chi Minh could rely on support from his fellow Communist across the northern border.

France now changed her policy. It was necessary to make a bid for the support of non-Communist nationalist elements in Vietnam: the French government signed an agreement in March 1949 with Bao Dai, the ex-Emperor of Annam who had abdicated in August 1945 and had spent most of the succeeding years in France. It was also necessary to bring in outside support: the French government induced the United States to send a mission and military supplies to Vietnam on the grounds that the colonial war had turned into an indirect struggle against the Communist Powers of Russia and China who had recognized Ho's government and that the front in Vietnam might well be the last that could be held against Communism in the whole of Southeast Asia.

The French change of policy came too late. Although the terms given to Bao Dai were a great deal more generous than those offered to Ho Chi Minh two or three years earlier, they still did not amount to independence, and there was little sign that the Vietnamese were content with them or even believed in France's intention to carry them out. To most people Bao Dai seemed a mere puppet of France. As for the Americans, they could be expected to send help but not to send military forces now that such intervention might be regarded as a *casus belli* by China and lead to a major war. Yet it was military forces that France needed; by 1951 her casualties included nearly 33,000 killed. In that year the French military position improved, thanks to the generalship of De Lattre de Tassigny, who regained much of the territory lost in Tonkin in 1949, but victory by French arms alone was out of the question and by 1954 it was obvious that even the Red River could not be held.

What had begun as a minor nationalist revolt had now turned into a matter of major concern to all the world's greatest powers. At a conference in Geneva held in the summer of 1954 and attended by the Foreign Ministers of the United States and Britain, of the Soviet Union and Communist China — a conference during the session of which the French garrison holding Dien Bien Phu was forced to surrender to Ho's forces — a cease-fire agreement was reached. The French were to evacuate Vietnam north of the 17th parallel, leaving Tonkin and northern Annam to the Vietminh. South of the parallel the French were to remain as supporters of Bao Dai's "independent" regime. An election was to be held by July 1956 throughout Vietnam, and the provisional government emerging from that was to decide the future status of the whole country.

The Geneva Agreement was a triumph for the nationalists under the Communist-led Vietminh. It provided for no United Nations supervision of the elections, and the Vietminh could in any case count on a majority, for the area they controlled included the greater part of the total population. Even in the south there would be a large Vietminh vote, or at any rate a vote against the parties which were being propped up by French forces and American money. By the end of 1955 it was clear that no elections would be held as laid down by the Geneva Agreement. The United States had refused to sign the political clauses of this agreement, and so had Mr. Diem, the Prime Minister of Southern Vietnam who was the United States protégé. Mr. Diem secured the deposition of Bao Dai by a referendum and got the French government's undertaking to withdraw their Expeditionary Corps. The Indochinese war had been a disaster for France. The drain of military man-power had left her unable to play her full part in European politics, the drain of money had weakened her efforts toward economic recovery at home and the loss of prestige gave the lie to her pretensions to be an imperial power elsewhere in the world.

INDONESIA

The Netherlands East Indies are one of the last places in the world where a successful nationalist movement might be expected. The islands are widely separated, the indigenous people are of many races (though mostly Malaysian) and of many religions (though mostly Moslem), and the Dutch, who had been established in some parts for over three centuries, had latterly been pursuing a liberal policy, imposing less of a color bar than other white rulers in Southeast Asia and appointing Indonesians to all but the highest places in the administration. But the fact remained that the Dutch were imperialists and gave the impression of regarding themselves as a superior people, and this was enough to create a desire for independence. The surrender of Japan and the circumstances of the few months following it gave the opportunity.

Japan surrendered, but Indonesia remained almost completely occupied by the Japanese. Responsibility for the whole area was suddenly shifted to Admiral Lord Louis Mountbatten's South-East Asia Command, which had hitherto been responsible only for Sumatra. Mountbatten did not have at his disposal enough ships, men, or knowledge. His officers found that a Republic of Indonesia had been proclaimed on August 17 and since it was not their business to interfere in internal politics they gave it what amounted to recognition. But they could not establish order, which it was their business to do. The Japanese were letting scores of thousands of rifles and thousands of machine guns fall into the hands of Indonesians, who used them in a flurry of murderous anarchy and in so far as they kept their powder dry at all kept it for use against the Dutch. When the Netherlands government's officials returned they found a nationalist spirit deeply implanted in the younger generation of Java and Sumatra and a nationalist republican government officially if inefficiently established in Jakarta.

This government consisted of nationalist leaders, some of whom had worked underground during the Japanese occupation and others who had pretended to side with the Japanese and to whom the Japanese had transferred some authority in the months preceding the surrender. At its head was Soekarno, an orator and natural leader who had suffered imprisonment and exile at the hands of the Dutch in the prewar years and had collaborated with the Japanese during the occupation. His ablest lieutenant, Hatta, had graduated from the University of Rotterdam, where he was already known as an Indonesian nationalist. Both were in their middle forties. Sjharir, the Republic's first Prime Minister, was even younger — he was born in 1909. He had studied law in Holland and

had become chairman of the Indonesian Labor League on his
return. Unlike his seniors he had refused any collaboration
with the Japanese. What they had in common was an inability to contemplate the return of Dutch authority in any
form whatever.

On the Dutch side negotiations were in the hands of Dr.
Van Mook, a Hollander born in Java. A better man for the
task could not be imagined, but he was handicapped by reactionary elements in the Netherlands government, as well
as by the inability or refusal of the Indonesian republican
government to implement any agreement that he might be
able to reach with them. Van Mook's idea was to recognize
the Republic as one among many states in Indonesia, all of
which would be linked more or less closely but not in a
colonial relationship with the Netherlands. He secured an
agreement in this sense at Linggajati in November 1946, but
when it was not implemented the Dutch turned to "police
action," a euphemism for military operations intended to re-
establish Dutch control over a wide area. This outraged not
only the Indonesians but also the Security Council of the
United Nations, which sent a Committee of Good Offices
to Java. The police action was called off and a truce signed
in January 1948. But the Dutch were in no mood to listen
to the United Nations for long, and by the end of the year
they had launched a second police action, overrunning the
Republican territory and interning Soekarno and other leaders.

This got the Dutch nowhere. Indonesia was still anarchic
and the anarchists who could agree on nothing else were
agreed that the Dutch must go. Negotiations were resumed
in 1949 and from a series of round-table conferences the Republic of the United States of Indonesia emerged. By The
Hague Agreement in December 1949 Indonesia became independent. To save the face of the Dutch, the Queen of the

Netherlands was given nominal headship of a so-called federation comprising the Netherlands, the Dutch West Indies and the Republic of Indonesia, but a few years later this fiction was dropped. In fact all that the Dutch kept in Indonesia was western New Guinea (Irian), a territory which could be of no use to them and little to the Indonesians, though it was important to both sides for prestige.

On paper nationalism was now triumphant: the Indonesian people had gained sovereignty. But everything else had still to be won. In 1950 none of the state governments in Indonesia was master in its own house. Most of them had no military power, and even in Java and Sumatra there were armed bands of outlaws which the government's forces could not overcome. Administrative mastery was ever farther to seek. The Republic was naturally short of trained administrators and even honesty was too much to expect of officials in a time of inflation and insufficient pay; it was estimated that nearly a third of the 1951 sugar crop disappeared through pillage. Opposition to the centralizing policy of the Jakarta government was strong, especially in the Celebes. In the political sphere Soekarno's National Party was faced with two ugly rivals. The first was the Moslem Party (Masjumi) which might not appear ugly but which had within it a fanatical religious faction capable of poisoning the whole body politic. The second was the Communist Party. It had been defeated in 1948 when it had tried, on orders from Moscow, to lead an insurrection which had been put down by the Indonesian government without need to call in Dutch help, but it had changed to a United Front policy which might be infinitely more dangerous. How strong this party was, no one knew. It was claiming 500,000 members in 1954, but that was almost certainly an overestimate. It was influential in the trade union organization (SOBSI), which counted 2,500,000 members, and it was trying to make up lost ground among the peasants by changing the party line from nationalization and collectivization of the land to "the establishment of individual peasant-proprietorship." As long as there was a Communist government in China and a million and a half Chinese in Indonesia, the Communist Party would continue to be a danger.

MALAYA

While Britain happily recognized Burma as a sovereign state and the Netherlands grudgingly admitted the independence of Indonesia and France suffered eviction from Indochina, Malaya remained throughout the postwar decade as part of the British Colonial Empire. For this there were two main reasons. One was that, as the largest producer of natural rubber in the world and the producer of half the world's tin supplies, Malaya was indispensable as a dollar-earner. Without the hundreds of millions of American dollars which Malaya earned every year and paid into the sterling pool, Britain would have had to halve her imports from the United States. There was a chance that a non-colonial Malaya would be equally lucrative, but it was not a risk that could be lightly taken. The other reason was that even if Britain had had the best will in the world to grant Malaya independence, none of the inhabitants except the minute Communist minority would have welcomed it. The people needed Britain's protection against the outside world and, more immediately, against each other. They were a plural society of Malays, Chinese, Indians and Eurasians, in which the largest single group were Chinese (44.7 per cent of the total population in 1947) and the second Malays (43.5 per cent, including "other Malaysians"). The widest differences of race, religion, language and temperament divided the Malay and Chinese communities, and to these were added an economic differentiation: the tin mines and most of the other productive property were owned by the Chinese, who also controlled most of the trade.

The problem facing liberal-minded Britons in Malaya after the war, was not, as it was in India, Ceylon and Burma, how and when to meet the demands of local nationalism. It was how to create a nation. The first superficial necessity was to bring some pattern into the patchwork constitution of Malaya, which, though a country no larger than England with under six and a half million inhabitants, was divided into nine states and a number of Straits Settlements, including Singapore. The proposal made in 1946 was to constitute Singapore (where 77.6 per cent of the population were Chinese) as a separate colony and to amalgamate the rest into a Malayan Union. This would have been to the advantage of the Chinese and was vociferously opposed by the Malays. The British government therefore changed its mind and in 1948 substituted a Federation of Malaya for the proposed Union. Under the Federation the Sultan of the states and their chief ministers were left more authority than before. Singapore remained separate, and there was even less pattern in the patchwork than there had been before the war.

At this point what become known as the Emergency arose in the form of a Communist insurrection. The Malayan Communist Party had distinguished itself during the Japanese occupation when it formed what it called the Malayan People's Anti-Japanese League — in reality a guerrilla force of Malayan-Chinese numbering between 3500 and 7000. Between the end of effective occupation and the arrival of British power in September 1945, the M.P.A.J.A. assumed control. It was December before it was disbanded. Then the Communists turned to pacific action through the trade unions: in January 1946 they led a strike in which 150,000 people stopped work for three days, but their attempt to stage a general strike in February was a failure. Now, in June 1948, they turned to a campaign of terrorism. If British official sources are to be believed, this was part of a concerted movement in Southeast Asia engineered by Russians who had attended the Communist Congress in Calcutta in the previous February.

The insurrection began with acts of terrorism on isolated estates in Johore and Perak. It was waged by guerrilla forces of perhaps 5000 fighters, helped by a civilian fifth column of anything up to 20,000 and dependent for food, supplies and replacements on settlements of Malayan-Chinese who had moved out of the towns during the Japanese occupation to squat on the fringe of the jungle. Although the guerrillas, the fifth columnists and the squatters were almost all Chinese, the Malayan-Chinese as a whole were as little sympathetic to Communism as were the Malays, Indians and Eurasians. They regarded the Emergency as the affair of the government, by which they meant the British, whose business it was to put an end to the Communist terror.

This the British were unable to do. Under their leadership 618 terrorists were killed and 337 captured in 1949, but civilian losses in the same year were 496, in addition to which 229 policemen and soldiers were killed. In 1950 the casualties mounted: 639 terrorists killed for the loss of 752 civilians and 94 police and military. By this time it was obvious that the Emergency could not be ended by fighting: the necessity was to stop the terrorists' source of supply. A scheme known as the Briggs Plan (after Lieutenant-General Briggs, who was appointed Director of Operations in April 1950) was put into operation to protect the jungle fringes and to bring the squatters under administrative control. It meant resettling the outlying squatter groups into compact new villages. Though never completed, the plan was successful in that it deprived the guerrillas of supplies and forced them to change their strategy. A Communist directive of October 1, 1951, ordered a shift of emphasis from shooting to infiltration. Isolated acts of terrorism nevertheless continued, the most distressing being the assassination of the High Commissioner, Sir Henry Gurney, on October 6.

With the appointment of General Sir Gerald Templer as his successor in January 1952, a new stage in British policy began. His directive stated that: "The policy of H.M. Government in the United Kingdom is that Malaya should in due course become a fully self-governing nation. H.M. Government confidently hope that that nation will be within the British Commonwealth." But during the period of Templer's administration, which lasted till June 1954, little was done to create that nation, let alone to make it self-governing. The Malay and Chinese communities were left as far apart as ever, and the latter were given much more reason to believe that Britain was favoring the Malays. In October 1953 the Malayan Civil Service included 239 permanent British officials, only 64 Malays and not a single Chinese. The ordinary people still had no share in electing the state and federal governments, and although after 1950 they had some share in electing local-government bodies, these were largely impotent. The whole concentration after Templer's appointment was on the Emergency, and Malaya was turned into a police state.

When 1955 came the Emergency was still not over. Communist guerrillas 5000 strong were still at large in the jungle and the Communist fifth column was still at work underground in the towns. The Communists had not succeeded in identifying themselves with a nationalist movement, but neither had the British. Malayan nationalism had not yet been born; a feeling of nationhood common to Chinese and Malays had not yet been created. But the British were ready now to allow general elections. In Malaya the Tengku Abdul Rahman became Chief Minister at the head of an alliance of the chief political parties of the Malays and the Chinese and with the aim of independence for Malaya by August 1957. In Singapore elections held in April 1955 led to a local government of members of the labor front and showed an urgent demand for Singapore's independence.

THE PHILIPPINES

Behind the movements for national independence in Southeast Asia was not only the impulse of the people to be free of the white man's imperialism but also the desire for social justice. The movements were social — one might almost say socialist — as well as nationalist; the enemy was the exploiter of the masses, whether foreign or native. This put the white man in a difficult predicament. If he was to have any success in his dealings with the nationalist movement, he must not merely come to terms with nationalism and abjure his imperialism; he must at the same time support a social revolution.

This necessity can be seen most obviously in the postwar history of the Philippines. There nationalism was born in the struggle against Spain in the nineteenth century. The United States annexed the islands in 1899 and proved itself the most liberal of rulers. By 1934 the Philippines Commonwealth had been set up with wide powers. In July 1946 its full sovereignty was recognized. There were perhaps limits to the independence of the Philippines — the United States secured the right to maintain military bases on the islands and insisted on privileges for American trade — but on the whole nationalism in the political sense was satisfied. The desire for social justice, on the other hand, was not. Unlike national leaders elsewhere in Southeast Asia, most of the Filipino leaders, whatever labels they might give themselves, were men of the Right, supporters with minor variations of the established social system. The Americans poured money into the Philippines after the war (some $140 million came in various forms of relief in 1945 and 1946) but the effect was that the rich Filipinos got richer and the poor got poorer. A report by an American financial mission (the Bell Report: Department of State, Far Eastern Series, No. 38, October 1950) gave a shocking and incontrovertible picture of governmental corruption and lack of social conscience. There was bound to be a movement for social revolution, and it was bound to be ugly.

The movement called itself Hukbalahap, a word standing for the Anti-Japanese People's Army. It consisted of peasants with some Communist leadership from Manila, and during the war acted both as a resistance force against the Japanese and as a revolutionary movement against absentee landowners in Central Luzon. After the war its Communist leadership became more pronounced and its enmity was extended from Japanese imperialists and native landowners to American imperialists and to the Filipinos who dealt with them so profitably. By 1950 the Anti-Japanese People's Army was calling itself the National Liberation Forces. By 1955 the movement was still in arms. The Hukbalahaps and the Filipinos of the ruling classes were still vying with each other as protagonists of the nationalist cause, but the issue between them was social rather than national. Nationalism in the Philippines had entered its second phase, turning from the anti-imperialist to the socialist. It is a transition that can be seen most clearly in the case of China.

CHAPTER 6

CHINA

THE TRIUMPH OF the Communists in China was the most important single event in the postwar decade. It affected the lives of more people than any other event in history (nearly a quarter of the world's population is Chinese); and it swung a balance of power against the capitalist nations in the Great Power conflict.

Looking back, the astonishing thing is that the victory of the Chinese Communists was not foreseen either by the Americans or by the Russians. The United States was deeply committed to alliance with the Communists' enemy, Chiang Kai-shek's government, during the war and Congress voted it grants of over $1583 million in the years after Japan's surrender. The Soviet Union signed a treaty with Chiang in 1945 and showed no sign of regarding the Chinese Communists as a safe bet until they had proclaimed their People's Republic in 1949.

Communists and Nationalists in China are essentially two wings of the revolution which was fledged in 1911. In the minds of Sun Yat-sen and the early revolutionary leaders, the revolution had a double purpose: it was intended to be both national and social. Its aim was to rid China both of foreign control and of the warlords, landlords and rich families of merchants and bureaucrats whose depredations on the masses had become proverbial. The slogan of the revolution was, and has remained, Sun Yat-sen's Three Principles: Nationalism, Democracy and the People's Livelihood. Nationalism meant "China for the Chinese" and the end of unequal treaties and concessionary rights. Democracy involved a change in the whole structure of Chinese society, which was based on hierarchical privilege and on family piety. The People's Livelihood meant raising the standard of living by land reform and industrialization. These Three Principles were to be achieved in three stages, first by the use of military force, then by a period of tutelage under the revolutionary party, the Kuomintang, to guide and educate the people toward the third stage of constitutional self-government.

In 1924 the Chinese Communists were admitted to the Kuomintang as individual members. They were a group of upper- and middle-class intellectuals who at that time had no mass following in China — and incidentally no contact with Russia — and who had founded the Chinese Communist Party simultaneously in China and Paris. Among the founders were Chen Tu-hsieu, a professor at the National University in Peking, Mao Tse-tung, a library assistant at the same university, Chou En-lai, who led the Paris group, and Chu Teh, who came from the landlord class and had had a military career before going abroad and being converted to Communism in Germany.

KUOMINTANG VERSUS COMMUNISTS

At first the Communists gave no trouble to the Kuomintang, whose new leader, Chiang Kai-shek, had been the favorite pupil of Borodin, the Russian agent employed by the Kuomintang to organize its training school for military officers. But when Chiang led the great northern march in 1926 and was in control of the cities of the Yangtse, the inevitable split came. The Communists were determined on an immediate social revolution, and in that determination they could count on a certain following in the country. Chiang insisted on consolidating the country first and on building up its capital resources, which would mean keeping on good terms with capitalist interests both at home and abroad. He expelled the Communists from the Kuomintang and launched a series of campaigns against their followers, campaigns which failed to liquidate them but succeeded in confining them to an area in the far northwest.

There Mao Tse-tung and the other surviving leaders established a rural society which could claim to be pursuing the Three Principles of the revolution. It was Nationalist in the sense that it was against all foreigners and seemed more ready than Chiang to fight the Japanese, whose invasion of Manchuria — China's eastern provinces — had begun in 1931. It was democratic at least in ways in which the Kuomintang, controlled by a group of rich families, was not. And it was working for the People's Livelihood by the destruction of landlordism while the Kuomintang was actually increasing and consolidating landlord's powers.

In 1936, when the incursion of the Japanese armies into China had gone too deep to be ignored any longer, the Communists and the Kuomintang reached an agreement to form a united front against the Japanese. From 1937 till the Japanese surrender in 1945 they fought on the same side, but never together. The Kuomintang was fighting a positional war in the south while the Chinese Communists were carrying on guerrilla warfare in the north; there was no cooperation between them. In the last stages of the war the Communist armies were in a position to take possession of cities of North China and Manchuria; they were prevented by the Americans, whose aid installed the Kuomintang in the north, and by the Russians, who recognized Chiang's claim to Manchuria while removing industrial installations from the Manchurian cities to the Soviet Union.

Civil war between the Communists and the Kuomintang (miscalled the Nationalists — they were no more nationalist than their opponents) had never ceased since 1927 in spite of the ostensibly united front of 1937–45. Once the Japanese were defeated it broke out in new fury, with the Kuomintang now at a serious disadvantage. Chiang had the full recognition of the three Great Powers, who were flattering his government by calling China the Fourth Great Power, and he had the advantage of American subvention on a colossal scale, but he had lost the support of the people. After nearly twenty years in power the Kuomintang had become corrupt and arbitrary to a degree without precedent even in Chinese history. It was not the Kuomintang's fault that the Chinese people were poverty-stricken or that the war against Japan had been severe and unconscionably expensive, but the government had done nothing to check a galloping inflation and seemed content to let the rich get richer while the poor got poorer. The Chinese Communists could claim with obvious justification now that they rather than the Kuomintang stood for the three principles of Nationalism, Democracy, and the People's Livelihood. They and not the Kuomintang had revolutionary ardor and discipline. They and not the Kuomintang had the masses with them.

The civil war raged from 1945 to 1949, the Communists gaining as much from desertions as from victories, as much from arms and equipment handed over by renegade Nationalists as by arms and equipment left behind in Manchuria by the Japanese and allowed by the Russians to fall into their hands. The United States government can have had no illusions about their protégés in the Kuomintang. General Stilwell, who was liaison officer during the Japanese war, had nothing but contempt for Chiang Kai-shek. General Marshall, who was in China throughout 1946 attempting to reconcile the two parties, had to admit failure and could not conceal his disgust with the Kuomintang. General Wedemeyer, whose report was published in September 1947, had no doubt about the corruption of the Kuomintang and the degree to which it had lost popular support, and he accused Chiang's government of apathy in combating economic decay and of seeking the solution of internal problems in outside aid. He saw the likelihood of Communist victory and the futility of attempting appeasement, but his recommendation was that the United States should give Chiang more financial, military and advisory aid. The State Department replied with a plaintive White Paper, objecting that "the United States Government could not virtually take over the Chinese Government and administer its economic and military affairs." Yet in 1948 President Truman got Congress to grant $463 million for China for twelve months, $338 million being for economic assistance and the rest for use as Chiang might think fit. Chinese paper currency at that time had fallen to three or four million yuan to the dollar.

THE COMMUNIST VICTORY

By the end of 1948 it was obvious that the Communists would win. In January 1949 Tientsin fell and Peking was on the verge of surrender. Shanghai was "liberated" in May. By the end of 1949, when Chiang had fled to Formosa with what remained of his party cadres and military forces, all China was theirs. The Communists proclaimed the People's Republic of China in October, and their government was recognized by the Soviet Union and Great Britain, though not by the United States.

It was a popular victory. The Chinese people were glad to see the last of the Kuomintang, and their first sight of Communist soldiers and officials in the great cities was surprisingly pleasant. The Communists came as liberators and actually behaved as liberators: there was no looting, no victimization. The soldiers were civil, the officials were soldierly. The new regime was obviously dictatorial, but there seemed no harm in that. It was encouraging that it should launch a drive against the Three Evils to which government employees, Communist as well as others, are heir — namely, corruption, waste and bureaucracy. The rulers called themselves Marxists but their Marxism was obviously Chinese rather than German or Russian. They left room for capitalists in China and there could be no reasonable resentment against their campaign against the Five Vices of private enterprise, the vices of bribery, tax evasion, theft of State property, cheating on government contracts and stealing information for private speculation. Government and people enjoyed a honeymoon period which lasted till the autumn of 1950, when China entered the Korean War. Then, in a panic fear of conspiracy, the Communists filled the prisons with suspects, millions of whom (two million, if we are to believe the report of the Minister of Finance in 1952) were liquidated.

The task of the Communist rulers was of appalling magnitude. They were responsible for more people than any other government in the world's history (the census figures of 1954 were to give a total of 602 million Chinese, of whom 11.7 million lived overseas), and the population was increasing at the rate of 12 million a year. There seemed to be none of the foundations for progress in the twentieth-century sense. The people were uneducated: nearly 80 per cent were more or less illiterate, and not more than a quarter of a million had been to a university or secondary school. The means of dealing with the most usual vagaries of the weather — drought and flood — did not exist. Nor did a system of transport and communications on which any improvement of the standard of living must depend: there were few roads and even before the war had devastated the railway system there were only 12,500 miles of railway. The Communists would have to begin everything almost from the beginning — devise a popular script as the basis for mass literacy, get dams built by manual labor with no equipment other than spades and baskets, lay roads and railways by pre-machine-age methods. In an article published on July 1, 1949, to commemorate the twenty-eighth anniversary of the Communist Party of China, Mao Tse-tung wrote:

> Much work still lies ahead of us. If we were walking down a road, our past work would not seem like more than the first step of a ten-thousand-li-march. The remnants of the enemy must still be wiped out. A grave task of economic reconstruction spreads out before us. Some of the things we are familiar with will soon be laid aside, and we will be compelled to tackle things with which we are not familiar. This means difficulties. The imperialists count upon our not handling our economic problems well. They stand on the sidelines and wait for our failure.

LAND REFORM

It would be by land reform that the Communist government would be judged, land reform which lay at the heart of the Third Principle of the revolution and which was the abiding passion of the Chinese people, some 85 per cent of whom gained their living by the land. The intention of the Communists in this respect had never been in doubt: it had been reiterated again and again since the party's foundation in 1921 and was reaffirmed in an official slogan in May 1946: "Those who own the land must work it." When it came into power the party set out to achieve this end in four phases. The first was the phase of Agitation. A key village was selected in each area and there Communist agitators were sent to all meetings of the villagers to denounce the local landlords. It was easy to stir up hatred against the landlords, less easy to get the villagers rather than the party agitators to denounce them, even less easy to extend the campaign from the selected village to other villages in the area, but successful agitation was a necessary prelude to the second phase, that of Classification. Communist policy was to have the country dwellers clearly divided in five classes: the land-lords, that is landowners who did no work but lived on rent and usury, the rich peasants who owned land some of which they worked themselves while they rented out or hired labor for the rest, the middle peasants who depended on "exploita-tion" for between 15 and 25 per cent of their annual income, the poor peasant who paid rent for all the land he tilled, and the laborer who neither owned nor paid rent for any land at all. This difficult classification was usually carried out by ac-clamation: a mass meeting of the village was asked to decide each man's class. Everyone was naturally anxious to be graded lower than his real status; everyone who was jealous of him was anxious to grade him higher. This phase opened the way to the real business of land reform, the phase of Confiscation and Redistribution. The principle here was that landlords should be stripped of land and property and that rich peasants should be deprived of land they rented out. Redistribution meant that peasants were to be given ownership of the land they were accustomed to till. The landlords' old title deeds and contracts for loans were ceremonially burned and the new holders were given land-holding certificates pending the issue of the new legal deeds.

The pace at which the land reform was carried out varied with local conditions and with the dictates of the government. As early as April 1949 the leaders seemed alarmed by the violence and chaos of the rural revolution: "Generally speaking," announced Mao and Chu Teh in an eight-point declaration, "reduction of rent and interest should be carried out first and land distribution later." Eight months later the *Yangtse Daily* was pointing out that "torture was repeatedly applied to the landlord during the class struggle . . . this sort of noisy and riotous procedure and blind tumultuous action would only scare away the masses, isolate oneself, and give the landlords a chance to increase their resistance. . . . It will certainly fail to realize the aims of land reform as completely as peaceful distribution of land." By June 1950 a new agrarian law was passed exempting rich peasants from redistribution and insisting that "the purpose of the agrarian program was not merely to do justice to the peasants but to increase production." But with the Korean War came a fear that landlords might find ways of collaborating with the enemy, and the campaign against them was accelerated. The Chinese Central News Agency was able to announce that by mid-1951 40 per cent of the total arable area in central and southern China had been confiscated from the landlords.

However far the land reform may have gone by 1955 — and there are no statistics on which anyone knowing the Chinese Communists would rely — two things were certain. The agrarian revolution had been carried farther in six years, and farther in the direction advocated by Sun Yat-sen and desired by the Chinese masses, than any regime but a Communist dictatorship could have made possible. On the other hand, the revolution had not yet been followed by any considerable increase in production; indeed all the available evidence pointed to an opposite conclusion. The land might now be owned by those who tilled it, but the new owners lacked the means to make it more productive. Addressing the first session of the National People's Congress on September 23, 1954, Chou En-lai said: "The growth of agriculture obviously falls behind the needs of the people and the State for agricultural produce"; therefore, he added, "we must gradually carry out the Socialist transformation of agriculture. That is, to change backward individual farming step by step to collective farming by reorganizing the peasants into mutual-aid teams and co-operatives on a voluntary basis."

Increased production depended on mechanization and it was on machinery that the Communist government lavished its greatest efforts. There could be no rapid expansion of industry without foreign capital, and since the capitalist powers could be neither desired nor expected to help Communist China in this, the government had to turn to Soviet Russia. By the Sino-Soviet Treaty of February 1950 Russia agreed to provide 300 million U.S. dollars for a five-year period. This could be but a drop in the bucket of China's needs, but it was infinitely better than nothing. Thanks largely to Russian machinery and technicians, China's output of crude steel in 1954 was rather more than twenty times its output in 1937; but even at Chou En-lai's estimate of the 1954 production (2,170,000 tons) China's output was still only one-eighth of that of Britain. After Sino-Soviet negotiations lasting for more than eight months, it was announced in September 1953 that 141 industrial enterprises, concerned for the most part with mining, engineering and electric-power generation, would be rehabilitated or newly constructed with Soviet aid. The Chinese government declared a Five-Year Plan to be beginning in 1953, but it did not disclose the target figures. Some evidence of these, appearing in the Moscow *Pravda*, permitted the conclusion that, were the plan to be successful, China by 1957 would rank second only to Japan among industrial countries in Asia, though its production of crude steel would be no higher than Japan's had been in 1930 and by world standards China would still be no more than a third-rate industrial power.

THE FOURTH GREAT POWER

Looked at from the standpoint of 1955 the first six years of Communist rule seemed a blessing to the Chinese people. Compared with Kuomintang rule it was incorrupt, purposive, even lenient. It had followed the Three Principles of Sun Yat-sen without deviation, although with Marxist road signs. Nationalism had triumphed: China was now wholly for the Chinese. Enemies might hold that the Communists had expelled the Americans only to fall into the clutches of the Russians, but that was not the way it appeared to the Chinese people. Soviet Russia had treated Communist China as an equal. The Soviet Union was an ally, and if it was also a patron, its patronage was limited. Russia made no claims on Chinese territory: in 1952 the Soviet government agreed to transfer to the Chinese People's government all rights over the Chinese Chanchun railway, and in 1954 to evacuate Port Arthur. Meanwhile Democracy, the second principle, had advanced. Not very far — China was under a party dictatorship, government was totalitarian, the period of political tutelage was not ended — but farther than under the Kuomintang. As for the People's Livelihood, the sincerity of the Communists in that direction was not for a moment in doubt; if there were any doubts about the efficacy of their methods, those were still felt rather in America than in China.

Whether it was the Communists' victory or the United States' refusal to recognize that victory which brought China into the forefront of the Great Power conflict will long be debated. Mao Tse-tung made no secret of his bond with Russia. In his article of July 1949 he wrote: "The Chinese people must either incline toward the side of imperialism or toward that of socialism. There can be no exception to this rule. It is impossible to sit on the fence; there is no third road. . . . Internationally we belong to the side of the anti-imperialist front, headed by the Soviet Union. We can only turn to this side for genuine and friendly assistance, not to the side of the imperialist front." But it was not through Russian intervention that Mao's armies defeated the Kuomintang in the years after Japan's surrender. It was not as minions of Russia that they drove the Americans back from the Yalu River in 1951. And it was nothing to do with Russia that Communist China came into dispute with the United States over Formosa.

The Formosa question was thought to have been settled in 1943 when Roosevelt, Churchill and Chiang Kai-shek met in Cairo and declared that "all territories which Japan has stolen from the Chinese, such as Manchuria, Formosa and the Pescadores, shall be returned to the Republic of China" — an agreement to which Stalin assented in 1945 at Potsdam. In accordance with this agreement Chiang sent General Chen Yi to take charge of the island when the Japanese surrendered, and it was natural and legal that he should take refuge there himself with the remnant of his forces when driven from the mainland by the Communists in 1949. No

198 THE NATIONALIST MOVEMENTS

doubt he would eventually have been driven out of Formosa as well had he not come under American protection. In July 1950 when the United Nations decided to oppose aggression in Korea, President Truman sent the Seventh Fleet to "neutralize" Formosa. The Chinese Communists claimed the island as theirs, since they were "the Republic of China"; Chiang claimed it as his since he regarded himself as still being the head of that Republic and was still recognized as such by the United States. For years the Communists were threatening to invade the island, while Chiang was threatening to invade the mainland. It seemed as if Formosa might become the detonating point of a third world war, with the United States dragged in the wake of Chiang into open conflict with China. The tension was eased only in December 1954 when Dulles got a written undertaking from Chiang not to attack the Chinese mainland without prior consultation with the U.S. government.

The point of view of the Formosans received little consideration in all this. There were perhaps seven million of them, all except for some 170,000 Malaysian aborigines being of Chinese race though speaking a language far removed from Mandarin Chinese and feeling themselves to be a separate people. To them the million Chinese emigrants from the mainland and the 600,000 troops who had come over with Chiang were foreigners. Chiang's rule was at first abominable to the Formosans. His first governor, Ch'en Yi, treated them despicably. There was a rebellion in February 1947 which the Kuomintang put down ferociously. Later Kuomintang behavior improved, and when American missions and money began coming into the island (the United States provided $138 million in nonmilitary aid alone during 1955) the Formosans' lot became more bearable. But they were still a pawn in the game, and in retrospect the fifty years of Japanese rule that had ended in 1945 seemed almost happy.

Public opinion in Britain, whose government had recognized the People's Republic in China, had little sympathy with the American point of view in Formosa. The American claim that Communist capture of Formosa would make a fatal breach in the U.S. Air Force's chain of defenses whose links were in Japan, Okinawa and the Philippines seemed farfetched. The United States' obligation to Chiang and his 600,000 troops in Formosa, many of whom but for America's attitude would have made their peace with the Communists years ago, was not understood. Formosa, which in 1949 had been a mere bone of contention in the Chinese civil war, had been transformed into a stake in the palisade containing Communism in 1950 and in 1955 was a source of friction not only between the Communist and the Western world, but between the American and British Allies.

Part Three

THE GREAT POWERS AT HOME

CHAPTER 1

THE SOVIET UNION

THE GERMAN INVASION of 1941 and the war that followed cost the Soviet Union more than twelve million lives. Military losses amounted to seven million and civilian losses to at least five million. It was officially estimated that twenty-five million people had been rendered homeless, that 70,000 villages and 1710 towns had been ruined and that one-third of the national wealth had been destroyed. Few countries have ever suffered comparable losses and preserved their machinery of government intact. The remarkable thing is that the Bolshevik regime survived and proved itself capable of leading the U.S.S.R. to recovery under its prewar leaders and along its prewar lines.

Stalin announced that the aim of the fourth Five-Year Plan (1946–50) was "to restore the afflicted districts of the country, to restore industry and agriculture to their prewar level and then to exceed that level to a more or less considerable degree." The primary task of feeding the people was complicated by an unprecedented drought and crop failure in 1946, and although this was compensated by a bumper harvest in the next year which encouraged the government to a premature removal of rationing in December 1947, there were still serious food shortages in the Soviet Union. The shortage of housing which had afflicted the Russian people ever since the Revolution was to continue. The urban population increased from sixty-one million in 1940 to eighty million in 1953; building could never keep up with the influx. The government was concentrating on industry, and it was in this field that most progress was made during the postwar decade.

INDUSTRIAL RECOVERY

In the areas which had come under German occupation, industrial recovery had not reached half its prewar level at the end of 1946. In the Donbas, where more than half of all the Soviet Union's coal had been produced, output was still only 80 per cent of prewar in 1949. But by 1948 gross industrial output for the Union as a whole was exceeding the 1940 level by 14 per cent, with particularly big increases in the coal, iron and steel industries which were now being developed in eastern areas, away from the vulnerable Ukraine. The fifth Five-Year Plan, beginning in 1950, aimed at an increase of 12 per cent every year in the combined output of the basic industries. In the first year the increase was 16 per cent, in the second 11 per cent, in the third and fourth 14 per cent. The chairman of the State Planning Committee declared that in 1955 industrial production as a whole would be three times greater than before the war.

Skeptical as one may be about Soviet official statistics and estimates, Russian industrial recovery after the war must rank as an outstanding achievement, particularly in view of the low productivity of labor and the claims on man power made by the armed forces. (Early in 1955 there were said to be 4,500,000 men in the Red Army and 800,000 in the Navy.)

The quality of Russian industrial products in general might be low, but in some respects they were remarkably high, as those who suffered from Mig fighting planes in the Korean War had reason to know. It was a surprise when the Russians succeeded in manufacturing atom bombs in 1949, and when Malenkov told the Supreme Soviet in August 1953 that the United States "had no monopoly in the hydrogen bomb" few people in the Western world believed him, though Western leaders had soon to admit that Russia had not only the bombs but the planes in which to deliver them.

AGRICULTURAL DEVELOPMENT

For the Bolsheviks agriculture has always been the most difficult problem and the peasant the most awkward customer. The Communist revolution on the land did not seriously begin until some thirteen years after the Revolution, and there was to be passive resistance, famine and wholesale deportation of "kulaks" before the collective-farm pattern could be established. On the collective farm, where the worker had to be left with his own plot of an acre or so, the tendency always was for him to put in more work on his private plot and less on the collective. The problem facing the Communist government was threefold: how to establish stronger Party control over the peasants, how to reduce the labor force on the land so as to find recruits for industry, and how to increase the yield of the collective farms so as to feed the fast-increasing urban population.

The first postwar attempt to solve this triple problem was a plan to combine the collective farms into larger units. The over-all aim was to reduce the number of collective farms to one-third. In 1950 and 1951 the great drive in this direction was made. It succeeded in reducing the number by about half: in 1950 there were perhaps 250,000 collective farms in the Soviet Union; by 1951 there were probably only 123,000. The process was carried farthest in the Moscow region, where the number was reduced from 6069 to 1668, and least far in regions most distant from the capital. Professedly the purpose was to make the use of agricultural machinery more effective and to facilitate the raising of a greater variety of crops on one farm, but the government had certainly two other motives in mind. The larger units made possible a release of man power, especially of administrative staff, for industrial work in the towns, and they also made for easier political supervision of the farm workers. The original collective farms had for the most part covered the land of a single parish. The workers lived in their old villages, felt their old parish loyalties and were inclined to work the land in their old ways. Now in the amalgamated farms they must in most cases move to new homes in what were called "collective-farm settlements," there to be enrolled in the "constant working brigades" dear to the bureaucrats' hearts — permanent gangs which were sent out to work in whatever corner of the vast new farm the manager might require their services. Now there could be a Communist cell or branch in each collective farm, which had never been possible before.

From the point of view of increased production the larger units seemed to yield no very satisfactory results. Khrushchev had to admit in September 1953 that agricultural production did not satisfy "the demands of the toilers" and that its increase between 1940 and 1952 had been no more than 10 per cent. In February 1954 he went farther: "The actual level of cereal production does not satisfy the growing needs of our national economy." Yet cereal production was the Soviets' greatest pride; everyone knew that the failure in meat and dairy production had been much greater.

The next step was to offer inducements. The collective farms had to pay in kind for the services of the Machine and Tractor Stations and they were handicapped by not knowing the amount of their debt until the bill came in; now in 1954 a reduction and flat-rate standardization of M.T.S. payments was announced. The collectives also had to make compulsory deliveries of produce in proportions and at prices fixed by the state; now the amount was to be reduced and the payment increased. Out of what was left, the collectives had to make contracts before harvest for sale to state and cooperative purchasing departments; now those contracts were to be more favorable to them. A further alteration was that each farm was to fix the minimum number of labor days to be done by each worker on the collective land, instead of having this fixed by the state.

These inducements, which were associated with the name of Khrushchev, were apparently not sufficient. The cereal harvest of 1954 brought in only 4 per cent more than that of the previous year. And something had gone wrong with the plan for stock-breeding: the actual increase in the number of cows, for instance, was 47 per cent lower than the increase estimated for the year ending October 1, 1954. Only industrial crops, notably cotton, showed a really satisfactory increase.

One reason for the lag in cereal production was that another step to increase production was being taken simultaneously. This was the New Lands Plan, which aimed at reclaiming anything up to thirty-two million acres of wasteland and virgin soil, mostly in Siberia and Kazakhstan. This meant a great diversion of capital equipment — tractors, plows, bulldozers, water piping, etc. — from the old grain-producing areas of the southwest and a considerable diversion of skilled labor. *Pravda* reported that as many as 50,000 voluntary workers went out to Machine and Tractor Stations in the new lands during the summer of 1954. What the New Lands Plan would eventually yield, no one could predict, but there seems to be no doubt that in the minds of the Soviet leaders at this time it was the most important project ever undertaken in Soviet agriculture.

OUTPOSTS OF EMPIRE

Perhaps the most remarkable of Soviet developments have been in the most distant quarters of the Union. For example we may take an area in the far north and one in the farthest south. Vorkuta lies between the Ob and Pechora Rivers in a region of arctic tundra which is frostbound for nine months of the year. Until Soviet surveyors found anthracite deposits in the region, it was uninhabited and considered uninhabitable. Then a railway was laid from Kotlas, eight hundred miles away, and while it was being completed, materials, machinery and labor were shipped from Archangel on the thousand-mile route to Khalmer-In, whence they were dragged a hundred and fifty miles across the snow to Vorkuta. By 1945 there were 30,000 people in the new settlement and five million tons of coal were being produced. By 1951 production was up to ten million tons. There was a new railway to Khalmer-In in the north and to the Ob delta in the east. Iron was being brought from the Kola Peninsula and a metallurgical plant was working at Vorkuta.

All this constituted a triumph of man over nature which has few parallels, but it was also a triumph of man over what we like to think of as human nature. The whole Vorkuta development was in the hands of the Political Police (M.V.D.). The labor involved was convict labor, rounded up by the Political Police and transported by them across the tundra. Technically these prisoners were serving sentences of two or seven years under Article 58 of the criminal code, but if they survived and were given their discharge, they were apt to be retained compulsorily as "free civilian settlers." How many convict laborers have died in Vorkuta there is no means of knowing with any accuracy. A Polish engineer, A. Eckart, who escaped in 1947, estimated that a million had died there by the end of 1946. There were whole tracts of the Union similarly under Political Police rule, states within the State, of which there is no evidence beyond that of a few released prisoners who succeeded in making their way to the Western world.

Tadzhikistan offers a more conventional example of Russian imperial development. A Soviet Republic of one and a half million people, Iranian in race, Moslem in religion, it lies in between the Altai Mountains and the Pamirs on the borders of Afghanistan and China. The Kremlin's object there was to modernize the people while securing their loyalty to the Communist regime. It was an enlightened task by imperialist standards and was carried out with no more brutality than its achievement within a single generation made necessary. Continuing the task they had begun before the war, the Russians set up five new Machine and Tractor Stations and vastly increased the yield of cotton and jute. They brought electric light and power to the towns, even to Khorog, the highest city in the Soviet Union. Literacy in the Tadzhik language was made almost general. There was some progress in teaching Russian as a second language, but here there were difficulties. Tadzhiks who could teach Russian were hard to come by. Girls were apt to marry, according to custom, before reaching the age for leaving a secondary school. Yet a State university was opened in 1948, and the Kremlin officials responsible for Tadzhikistan could pride themselves on having achieved educational and economic progress which perhaps no other imperialists could have reached in so short a time. It was not the work of the Political Police. If it was largely the work of Russians, that was not because of any racial policy, but because there were not yet enough Tadzhiks trained to fill the responsible posts.

The map of Soviet development in the postwar decade was studded with these incongruities. Here a piece of enlightened imperialism; there a convict settlement where the barbarities almost exceeded credibility. Here — as in the New Lands Plan — a project which brought thousands of young people out from the European cities to make the eastern wastelands blossom like a garden; there a policy of deliberate genocide such as that practiced in the Baltic Republics of Estonia, Latvia and Lithuania. The end was the same in all cases — the securing and strengthening of the Soviet Union; the means employed in the postwar years were no different from those which had been used ever since Stalin had come into power.

AFTER STALIN

When Stalin died on March 5, 1953, there was no one to take his place, no one man who was able to control as he had controlled for decades the three great forces in the Soviet Union — the Party, the Army and the Political Police. When he was gone, power resided with four men, namely Malenkov, Bulganin and Beria, the respective heads of these three forces, and Molotov, who had been in charge of Soviet foreign policy since 1939. To these were added a fifth, Khrushchev, who took Malenkov's place as Secretary-General of the Communist Party when the latter succeeded Stalin as Prime Minister. They described themselves as forming a collective leadership, but there was no question of the Party, the Army and the Political Police having anything approaching equal powers.

Everything had to be subordinated to the Party, and the dangerous rival to the Party was not the Army — Bulganin was not a soldier but a party-man who had been put in charge of the military machine — the danger came from the Political Police. It was necessary, therefore, to get rid of Beria: he was dismissed in July 1953, put on trial and executed, and in his place was put a sound policeman, Kruglov, who had no political talents or position. After a thorough purge of Beria's nominees, the Political Police could no longer be considered a danger to the remaining collective leaders.

More serious dangers remained. No one could know what course the Soviet peoples might take deprived of Stalin's leadership, and there was some reason to fear that the satellite nations might take Stalin's going as an opportunity to break the bonds with which he had tied them to the Soviet Union. There was the possibility that the capitalist powers might seize the chance to attack the Soviet Union before Stalin's successors were firmly in the saddle. It was necessary for "collective leadership" to make an immediate bid for popularity. This took the form of a policy that was called the New Course, the tenor of which was that there was to be a concentration on producing consumer goods. As *Soviet News* put it: "The Soviet people deprived themselves of many things and the State economized on everything in order to invest bigger sums in the development of heavy industry. This task has now been successfully accomplished and the country can, in real earnest, undertake the development of those branches of the economy which satisfy the consumer demands of the people." Addressing the Supreme Soviet, Malenkov said that it was "essential to increase investment in the development of light industry and to draw the engineering and heavy industries on a wider scale into consumer-goods production."

To the Soviet peoples the New Course seemed to spell more

food, clothing, household utensils and amenities of all sorts. The satellite peoples could interpret it as an easing of pressure on their own heavy-industry expansion and as permission to concentrate on consumer-goods production for themselves. The capitalist powers could note that less stress on heavy industry in Russia would mean less concentration on armaments production. This reassurance was encouraged during 1953 and 1954 by Molotov's talk of "peaceful co-existence" and by some relaxation in the Kremlin's attitude toward the West. More Western delegations were invited to visit the Soviet Union; more artists and athletes were sent from Russia to perform in the capitalist world. Firmer grounds for reassurance were given when Molotov used his influence to promote armistice in Korea and Indochina.

The New Course served its purpose in tiding Stalin's successors over the dangerous period following his death, but from any other point of view it was a failure. The United States and British governments were not impressed by "peaceful co-existence"; they continued to increase their own armaments and to work for the rearmament of Western Germany. Meanwhile something had gone very wrong with the plan to produce more consumer goods in the Soviet Union. This plan depended on the switching over of part of the existing heavy-industry plant to light industry, but the demands of the armed forces and the needs of the "new lands" made this impossible. It depended also on increased production from the farms, which was not in fact forthcoming. The collective farmers had been given a reduction in taxes and an increase in prices offered for their foodstuffs, but all this was no inducement; if there were no more goods for them to buy, there was no point in their having more money.

At the beginning of 1955, therefore, the New Course was abandoned. Concentration was shifted back to heavy industry, as in Stalin's day. The 1955 budget showed an expenditure of 163,604 million rubles on heavy industry compared with 133,214 million in the 1954 budget; expenditure on light industry was reduced from 36,570 million in 1954 to 27,935 million; defense expenditure showed an increase of 12 per cent. For the failure of the New Course there had to be a scapegoat. The obvious person for this role was Khrushchev, who had had a special responsibility for agriculture, but as head of the Party he must be above suspicion. The lot fell to Malenkov, who declared to the Supreme Soviet his responsibility for the agricultural failure and resigned from the Prime Ministership, in which post Bulganin succeeded him. Khrushchev remained obviously in control of the Party; probably in control of the State. But if the New Course had been abandoned, the slogan of "collective leadership" had not. Soviet citizens were encouraged to put the blame for pre-1953 misfortunes on the one-man dictatorship of Stalin.

The postwar decade was the longest period of calm and stability that Russia had known since the Revolution. Throughout those years there was no threat of invasion, no actual famine, no need for a really major purge. The death of Stalin did not shake the regime, and the removal of Beria was carried out without serious repercussions. Compared with the starvation, the economic upheavals and the anti-kulak campaigns of the 1920's, compared with the agrarian revolution, the Hitler threat and the great purges of the 1930's, compared with the horrors of war in the early 1940's, the age which began in 1945 was a haven of peace. As such it will be rememberd by Russians, though the outside world may take a different view.

CHAPTER 2

THE UNITED KINGDOM

W HEN THE WAR ended, the British people were conscious of two needs. The first was the need to pay their way. They were wholly dependent on imports from abroad and now their capacity to pay for these imports had gone. "We fought this war," wrote Lord Keynes in 1945, "on the principle of unlimited liability and with more reckless disregard of economic consequences than others more fortunately placed." Huge debts had been incurred; capital assets of every sort, from reserves of gold and dollars and foreign investments to a great part of the shipping fleet, had been lost. It was clear that imports would have to be cut down, that there must be a great increase in home investment and that industrial effort must be concentrated on the export market. Years of hardship lay ahead, but the prospect did not make the British people despondent. With the aftermath of the First World War in mind, they knew that peace did not necessarily mean prosperity.

The second conscious need was for social justice. Memories of the between-war period were bitter, especially on the count of unemployment. No political party would get many votes unless it stood for full employment and offered a good prospect of redeeming its pledge. Memories of the wartime period were happy at least in one respect: it brought a diminution of class privilege, a much greater equality of opportunity, a sense of share-and-share-alike. Thanks to rationing and full employment no one had gone hungry; it was probable that the poor, and certain that the children of the poor, were better fed during the war years than they had been before.

Perhaps it was consciousness of this second need which led to the victory of the Labour Party in the elections of July 1945. The war had been fought under a coalition government with Churchill, the Conservative leader, at its head and Attlee, the Labour leader, as Vice-Premier. It was recognized as a good government, but few people wanted a continuance of coalition in peacetime. The parties contested the elections in rivalry and although Churchill was at the height of his prestige and popularity, the Conservatives and their associates won only 213 seats to Labour's 393. For the first time in its history the Labour Party came into office with a clear parliamentary majority.

THE WELFARE STATE

The two great achievements of the Labour government were the nationalization of certain basic industries and the establishment of what came to be known as the Welfare State. Neither was very seriously opposed by non-Labour opinion. The basic industries had been operated on a national basis during the war; it was not administratively difficult or constitutionally shocking to put them permanently under State ownership and control. Nationalization of industry was a socialist doctrine, but by the way it was carried out the vice itself lost half its evil by losing all its grossness. The railways, the coal, gas and electricity industries, civil aviation, Cables and Wireless Ltd., and the Bank of England were nationalized and acts were passed for the nationalization of the steel and road-haulage industries, but shareholders were compensated on a generous scale and many of the prominent figures in the old private companies found places side by side with trade union leaders on the boards which were set up to control the national organizations.

There was a smack of socialism about the Welfare State, but in fact its principles owed as much to Conservatives and to Liberals as to Labour politicians. A Liberal, Sir William Beveridge, had drawn up during the war a Report on Social Insurance and Allied Services, and this had been accepted, with some changes, by the Coalition government; it was to be the basis of Labour's welfare legislation. Another Liberal, Eleanor Rathbone, had campaigned for family allowances, and the Coalition government had put through the Family Allowances Act, though it did not come into force until 1946. (It was not a far-reaching measure — five shillings a week for every child under sixteen years of age except the first — and the Labour government carried it no farther, for the increase to eight shillings, after March 1952 hardly made up for the increased cost of living.) A Conservative, R. A. Butler, was the minister responsible for the great Education Act which was passed under the Coalition government in 1944.

The principles were thus laid down; all the Labour government had to do was to apply them. But in the penury in which Britain found herself after the war that task needed great courage and determination. The Education Act provided for free full-time secondary education for all up to the age of 16 and for part-time education in new County Colleges between the ages of 16 and 18. For this there were neither the buildings nor the teachers. The utmost that could be done

in the postwar decade was to raise the school-leaving age from
14 to 15 and to see that there were places and teachers for
every boy and girl in one of the three types of secondary
school — grammar, technical or modern — according to ability shown in an examination taken at the age of eleven.
Socialist principles might have led the Labour government to
abolish the private schools, preparatory and "public," to
which well-to-do parents were inclined to send their children;
but these schools were left as they were. The universities remained as they had always been in Britain, independent of
State and local-government authority. What was changed
was the amount of public money which was poured into them.
The number of university students almost doubled in the
years after the war, and the majority of them were aided by
grants from one source or another. What happened in the
postwar years was a rapid progress toward equality of opportunity for education, a direction in which England had
hitherto lagged behind most other democratic countries.

Welfare in the narrower sense was promoted by four Acts
of Parliament which came into operation in 1948. The least
well known of these was the Children's Act, "to make further
provision for the care or welfare, up to the age of 18 and, in
certain cases, for further periods, of boys and girls when they
are without parents or have been lost or abandoned by, or
are living away from, their parents, or when their parents are
unfit or unable to take care of them." The other three are of an
importance which will make them landmarks in the social
history of Britain. The National Insurance Act provided
insurance for every British citizen in the form of benefits to
meet every likely form of need — unemployment, sickness,
maternity and widowhood, as well as guardians' allowances,
retirement pensions and death grants. The National Assistance Act provided especially for the care of old people and for

supplementing national insurance benefits by noncontributory pensions and other means so as to bring them up to a level necessary for decent subsistence. The National Health Service Act, which proved the most controversial of the four because of initial resistance by members of the medical profession, provided for free comprehensive medical service for all who wished to avail themselves of it. This involved a reorganization of existing health services of many varieties and the adoption of two new principles: hospitals were nationalized and free medical services were made available to the entire population instead of only to insured persons as in the past.

Like the Education Act, the new Health Service came into operation at an unfortunate time. For the first there were not enough teachers or schools, for the second there were not enough doctors, oculists, dentists or nurses to meet the demand of patients who were now applying for treatment to make up for a lifetime of medical neglect. There were not enough hospitals and clinics, and years must pass before new ones could be put up. For this building Britain could not spare the labor or the materials. First dwelling houses had to be built and repaired, to make up for the wartime neglect and damage from air raids and to accommodate the rising population. New factories had to be constructed, particularly for the industries engaged in producing for export. At this time there was a shortage of almost every raw material and article needed in the building trade.

YEARS OF AUSTERITY

Austerity, a word made current if not popular by Sir Stafford Cripps while Chancellor of the Exchequer (1947–50), was the keynote of the first six postwar years. Economic controls imposed during the war were maintained and in some cases tightened. In order to cut down imports, rationing was continued and on a more severe scale than at any time during the war. Bread was rationed for the first time in July 1946. It was 1949 before clothes and textile rationing ended, and during that year the meat ration was cut down to one shilling's worth a week, the sugar ration was reduced to eight ounces and candy rationing was resumed after having been lifted for a time. Taxation reached new heights. Income tax was stepped up, especially in the higher-income ranges, until as an American journalist Theodore H. White wrote, "Where before the war Britain could count some seven thousand people who kept incomes of £6000 (then worth approximately $24,000) or over after taxes, the Britain of today counts only sixty people who still retain £6000 (now worth $16,800)." Indirect taxation was increased, particularly in purchase-tax and in duties on beer, spirits and tobacco. Presenting the budget in 1948, Sir Stafford Cripps announced that receipts from taxation were likely to be £3.5 thousand million instead of £3.3 thousand million as in the previous year; it would be by far the highest taxation that had ever been imposed on the country. On top of these burdens came the strain of working against time for increased output in the export industries.

The British people accepted all this with a serenity which surprised foreign visitors and aroused their admiration. They saw drab towns, ill-lighted, unpainted and with bomb damage unrepaired, and shabbily dressed, rather gray-faced people. But if they noticed the babies and children they could not help finding them as healthy-looking as any they had seen elsewhere; if they looked at the countryside they found that agriculture was being revolutionized and that Britain's had become the most highly mechanized in the world; if they visited what in the 1930's had been the Distressed Areas they discovered a working class in full employment with a level of real family wages exceeding all precedent. They realized that Britain had concentrated benefits where they were most needed — on the coming generation, on food production, on the laboring people. The wealthy had suffered and so had the middle classes — in particular the professional class, for whom being deprived of domestic servants meant a revolutionary change — but there was no feeling that the rest had won a victory in a class war. The British people were proud to think that they were sharing their sacrifices and that there was now less material difference between the classes than in most other countries of which they had any knowledge.

THE DOLLAR SHORTAGE

If Britain were to pay her way and to achieve an acceptable standard of living, it was estimated by the government that exports must reach a level 75 per cent higher than before the war. By rationing, taxation, the allocation of raw materials and other controls it was easy to keep a high proportion of Britain's output off the home market; easy, for instance, to send three-quarters of the output of motor cars and whisky as exports overseas. The difficulty was to increase output when so many of the materials needed in the manufacture of industrial exports had to be imported from dollar countries — Canada and parts of Latin America as well as the United States — and to be paid for in exports for which a sale must be found in those countries. The United States loan known as Lend-Lease came to an abrupt end in August 1945, and although an agreement was signed in December to provide a credit of $3750 million at 2 per cent interest, it was July 1946 before this was approved by Congress. In the interim

Britain had to pay for all the supplies she was to receive from the United States.

Recovery was set back by an accident of the weather. The first months of 1947 brought snow, ice and floods; it was the worst winter Britain had known for sixty-six years. There was a shortage of coal and a consequent drop of £200 million in exports. Meanwhile American wholesale prices had risen by 50 per cent, thereby reducing the value of the new loan. A clause in the loan agreement obliged Britain to make her currency convertible, and when this was implemented in July there was a run by Britain's customers on her dollar resources which reached such an extent that convertibility had to be suspended in August. Britain was saved from what looked like financial ruin only by increased American aid under the Marshall Plan.

Nineteen-forty-eight was a good year and in January 1949 Sir Stafford Cripps was able to say that Britain was making nearly enough goods to buy all she required, though she was not finding the solution to the problem of selling enough in dollar markets. The next six months saw a very slight economic recession in the United States which was enough to upset Britain's balance and to bring on a financial crisis even more serious than that of 1947. It was found necessary to devalue the currency: in September 1949 the dollar value of the pound was reduced from 4.03 to 2.8. Then financial recovery set in, even more rapidly than the crisis. The Korean War led to stockpiling in the United States and to an increased demand for exports from the sterling countries. Whereas the combined sterling area had a deficit of $1511 million in 1949, it showed a surplus of $805 million in 1950. Britain was able to call an end to Marshall Aid two years before that end was due.

But the dollar crises of 1947 and 1949 were followed by a

third in 1951, when the dollar deficit reached $1164 million. This time it had to be met by a Conservative government with Churchill at its head and R. A. Butler as Chancellor of the Exchequer. The elections of 1950 had reduced the Labour majority to a mere eighteen and those of 1951 had led to a narrow victory for the Conservatives who, with their associates, won 321 seats in the House of Commons to Labour's 294. The Conservatives immediately did what Labour would have had to do in their place: they restricted imports and brought all steel sales under the strictest control.

BRITAIN'S RECOVERY

Anyone who expected that a Conservative government would seek to undo the apparently revolutionary legislation of its predecessor was soon to be disillusioned. Nationalization of the railways and coal, gas and electricity industries had come to stay; only in the steel industry and in trucking did the Conservatives upset Labour's intentions. The principles of the Welfare State were now almost as acceptable to Conservatives as they had always been to Socialists, and no attempts were made to restrict the implementation of the Education Act or of the four great Acts for social security. A recovery took place in Britain after 1951, but it was the cumulative result of hard work and managerial skill in the industrial field rather than of any change in government ideology. There was also a piece of good fortune. The terms of trade which had been against Britain till the end of 1951 now turned in her favor: during 1952 and 1953 world prices for British exports rose more than world prices for British imports.

The target which Britain had set herself for exports — an increase of 75 per cent over the prewar level — was exceeded in 1950, when it reached a 77 per cent increase and would be further exceeded in each following year. This made possible some gradual relaxation of controls and a cautious and piecemeal abolition of rationing. By the end of 1954 — the year which saw the end of food rationing and building licenses — the main body of controls over the home economy had been removed. According to the official *Economic Survey* (1955), "At home, 1954 was a successful year for the United Kingdom. Production continued to rise, living standards rose, there was an increase in the rate of industrial investment, and a high level of personal saving was maintained. In overseas trade and payments the United Kingdom again earned a substantial surplus on current account in the year as a whole; if defence aid is excluded, the surplus was about the same as in 1953."

All this made the British public inclined to be pleased with the Conservative government. Churchill felt confident enough to relinquish the Prime Ministership to Eden in April 1955, and at the general election held in the following month the Conservatives increased their over-all majority to 68.

THE NEW BRITAIN

The postwar decade saw the end of many of the conceptions which the British had held about themselves, and some of those which foreigners had held about Britain. The realization that the United Kingdom was not, in comparison with the Soviet Union or the United States, a Great Power involved a difficult psychological as well as political adjustment. Britain, it was now seen, could no longer hope to be able to defend herself alone. It was a revolution in Britain's policy when she committed herself to long-term military alliances first in the Dunkirk, then in the Brussels, then in the North Atlantic Treaties. It was contrary to all Britain's traditions that she should impose compulsory military service on her sons when war was not in immediate prospect: conscription for a period of twelve months came into force on January 1, 1949, and later was increased first to eighteen months, then to twenty-four — a longer period than any other European NATO country except Turkey was obliging her boys to serve.

While foreign and military policy was being revolutionized, the conception of Commonwealth was changing out of all recognition. The British people were far from sure what the Commonwealth was. It was no longer an association of peoples who were in any real sense British. Until 1947 the majority of Commonwealth citizens had been descendants of men and women who had emigrated from the British Isles. After 1947 the majority of Commonwealth citizens were Indians; it was a colored Commonwealth and the prevailing tone was dark. It was no longer a Commonwealth with a common King or Queen; India and Pakistan were republics. It was no longer an Association of States with a common political ideal: the South Africa of Malan and Strijdom repudiated the ideal of racial equality which was the professed creed of the other Dominions. It had never in peacetime been an association of states in political alliance, but now Australia and New Zealand were in military alliance with the United States (the Anzus Pact of 1951) rather than with the United Kingdom, and two other Commonwealth members, India and Pakistan, were in arms against each other over Kashmir. Nor was there any unity in foreign policy, for India was opposed to the policy of Containment. And it could no longer be said that members of the Commonwealth had more in common with each other than they had with any other countries. This was hardly true of Canada, which depended economically and militarily on the United States rather than on the United Kingdom, and not at all true of Britain herself, which had more in common with independent Ireland, for instance, than she had with any Commonwealth member.

Changes in foreign and imperial relationships naturally concerned the British people less than changes in class relationships at home. The Nazi propagandist Goebbels used to call Britain a plutocracy; whatever truth there may have been in that description in the 1930's, there was very much less in the 1940's. The ruling class had been supplemented by Labour leaders, many, though by no means all, of whom were workingmen's sons, and the educational facilities opened by the 1944 Act would bring many more poor men's sons to the top in a host of capacities in the next generation. Whether the government were Conservative or Labour, a large measure of power now lay in the hands of trade union officials, working-class leaders who soon learned the truth of what Macaulay had called "the English doctrine that all power is a trust for the public good." Britain was becoming more egalitarian. It might be argued that in the between-war years the gulf between rich and poor was widening, but there was no doubt at all that in the postwar years it was narrowing. Any fear there might have been that egalitarianism and the extension of government control or interference would smother the genius of the British people and stifle enterprise seems to have been disproved by the rate at which new industries developed — new aero-engines, new radio equipment, new synthetic textiles — and by the pace at which exports were increased. It appeared that Britain had met the postwar challenge not unsuccessfully.

CHAPTER 3

THE UNITED STATES

THE WAR WHICH did so much to damage the economies of the Soviet Union and the United Kingdom stimulated that of the United States, bringing to an end the great depression which had dragged on throughout the 1930's and intensifying production to a degree which would have seemed impossible in prewar days. Between 1939 and 1944 the output of agriculture was increased by a third, that of raw materials by two-thirds, and the production of manufactured goods trebled.

To the outside world the United States seemed to be in a condition of fabulous prosperity, but the average American did not see it like that in 1945 and 1946. He was conscious of housing shortages and even, when rationing was abruptly abandoned, of food shortages. Industrialists and agriculturists were irked by price controls and labor by wage limitations. Before the end of 1945 the cost of living had risen twice as much as hourly wages had done, and half a million workers were out on strike. In the coal industry strikes were so serious that the government had to take over the mines for a time in the summer of 1946. While trade unionists were withholding their labor, cattle-raisers, waiting for an end of controls, were withholding their beasts, and for some weeks there was a meat famine. The Administration seemed inept, and few people in those first postwar years had any confidence in the President. Truman had seemed a frivolous choice even for the sinecure of the Vice-Presidency and he had shown no signs of being of presidential timber when Roosevelt's death in April 1945 moved him to the White House.

The mood of the people may be gauged by the appeals made to them by the chairmen of the two great parties on the eve of the elections for the Eightieth Congress in the autumn of 1946. The Democrats' chairman said: "The issue is fundamentally this: shall Americans continue to go forward under the progressive program developed by the Democratic Administration for the benefit of *all* the people, or shall we surrender to the will of the few who want only large profits for themselves? In this election, the American people must choose between a party which offers a positive program of action and a party which offers no program at all." The Republican chairman said: "There are two issues: houses or blueprints, sound currency or inflation, government by majorities or pampered minorities, abundance or shortages, balanced budgets or deficit spending, Americanism or Communism, full production or restricted production, free economy or planned economy." The Republican appeal proved to be the more telling: they won a majority in both the Senate and the House of Representatives. They were now in a fair position to hamstring the President. Perhaps it was thanks neither to the Republican Congress nor to the Democratic administration that things went so well during the following years, when production continued to soar, unemployment dwindled and the purchasing public had money enough to buy the motor cars, radio sets and housing equipment which were pouring from the factories.

When the time came for the presidential elections in

1948 it was generally expected by political pollsters and commentators that Truman would be defeated by the Republican candidate, Governor Dewey. There was a third candidate in the field, Henry Wallace, whom experts reckoned would win five million votes. On both counts predictions were proved wrong. Wallace, preaching a radical, collectivist, pacifist, pro-Russian gospel, secured only about a million votes. Truman, promising an extension of the New Deal and of the Social Service State and a civil-rights program, including equal status for the Negro before the law and in the labor market, defeated Dewey for the Presidency. The Democrats won the congressional as well as the presidential elections, gaining twelve seats in the Senate and about eight in the House of Representatives.

Yet Truman found it no more easy to put across his domestic reforms during his second term of office than during his first. The public were calling for a halt in controls and social experiment, and Congress was hostile to any new measures of the Fair Deal — Truman's version of the New Deal of his predecessor. What his seven years' Presidency will be remembered for is not the Fair Deal but the revolution in foreign policy, political and economic, which did so much to maintain the boom conditions of the war years and to establish the United States in its role as a Great Power.

THE END OF ISOLATION

There was no question of returning after 1945 to the between-war policy of isolation. Americans had realized the mistake they had made in trying to disinterest themselves in Europe after the First World War, when Congress refused to ratify the Treaty of Versailles, the Covenant of the League of Nations and the Tripartite Treaty for the guarantee of

France, and when their army of occupation was withdrawn from the Rhineland, a separate peace was signed with Germany and futile attempts were made to insist on the payment of war debts. The events of 1941–45 had taught them that they could be attacked in American territory in the Pacific, that the British Fleet could never again be strong enough to defend the Atlantic approaches and that the polar air routes had brought American cities within range of potential enemies. Before the war ended they were resigned to a policy of involvement, supporting the conception of the United Nations Organization, whose headquarters were to be established on their territory. There were still isolationists in the United States, particularly among Republicans, but the form their isolationism took was "Asia first," favoring commitments across the Pacific rather than across the Atlantic. The Republican Party as a whole was not isolationist even in this sense, and the Republican Senator Vandenberg gave the staunchest support to President Truman and the State Department in what became a bipartisan policy of involvement.

In foreign policy, therefore, Truman had virtually his own way, and it was a way which his successor would not attempt to reverse. It is best remembered for five decisions, three of which seemed to have been taken on the spur of the moment. First there was the Truman Doctrine (see page 29), proclaimed as a basis for American participation in the defense of Greece and Turkey. Then came his support of the Marshall offer which was to do more than anything else to establish the United States' new role in Europe. When Russia advertised her antagonism to her allies by closing the land and water routes to Berlin from the west, Truman decided to break the blockade by airlift. From this he went on to sign the North Atlantic Pact. Finally came the snap decision to send American forces to fight in Korea. Altogether Truman's decisions added up to a policy of global intervention which would have been unimaginable by Americans a generation earlier.

FOREIGN AID

Professor Edward Mead Earle, writing in 1951, said of the Marshall Plan that

> it was a spectacular example of a fundamental Anglo-American principle of statecraft — enlightened self-interest. The Government and the people of the United States believed with conviction and sincerity that Europe could survive as free and independent only if recovery were prompt and thoroughgoing. And since they believed that their own freedom was contingent upon the survival of free institutions and political independence in Europe, they were willing to invest, to stake, more than $10 billion in European recovery. Seen in retrospect, this was the most profitable investment, as well as the largest, which the people of the United States ever have made in their own security and national interest.

Europeans were more conscious than ordinary Americans of the national interest aspect of the Plan. To Europeans it was obvious that the United States could not avoid a slump except by exporting, and since there was little that Americans wanted to buy from Europe in return for her exports, the United States in its own interest must give these exports away. There was an impatience to see the United States adapt itself to its position as the world's richest country "by adopting," as a French critic insisted, " a creditor mentality, which would involve a policy of foreign investment, increased exports, resignation to a deficit in the balance of trade and renunciation of a long tradition of protectionism."

This impatience was surely unjustified. Europeans were asking the Americans to adapt themselves in half a decade to a role which Britons had taken half a century or more to understand. It should have been obvious as soon as the Napoleonic wars were over that only by free trade, a single-currency system and by investment in backward areas could Britain play her part as the world's workshop, the world's carrier and the world's financier. But free trade took a long time in coming: it was 1846 before the British Parliament would repeal the Corn Laws and 1860 before a British government would sign a commercial treaty with France. It was the last quarter of the century before the Gold Standard was properly established; and as for investment in backward areas, the colonies had to wait until 1899 before the British Treasury was empowered to lend them money, and till 1900 before trustees were allowed to invest in colonial stock. If the United States was slow in making similar adaptation, no one should have been surprised. Delay would be more calamitous now that the world was so much more dependent on international trade, but the Americans had none of the Britons' inducement to think in terms of world commerce, for their country was virtually self-sufficient and in 1938 exports had amounted to little more than 10 per cent of their total production. The wonder was not that they kept to their tous now that the world was so much more dependent on imports, but that they poured out foreign aid with a readiness which was no less altruistic for being in their own interest.

As the Communist menace loomed larger, foreign aid for developmental assistance was outpaced by aid for military purposes, and this together with the large-scale rearmament program launched in 1950 and the exigencies of the Korean War kept the American economy booming by renewing the wartime stimulus to industrial expansion. But there were types of foreign aid much more modest in amount and more purely altruistic in intention which were not designed to bring any immediate material benefit to Americans. The best known of these is Point Four (later named the Technical Co-operation Administration), announced by President Truman in his inaugural address on January 20, 1949:

> Fourth, we must embark on a new bold policy for making the benefits of our scientific advances and industrial progress available for the improvement and growth of underdeveloped areas. . . . Our aim should be to help the free peoples of the world, through their own efforts, to produce more food, more clothing, more materials for housing and more mechanical power to lighten their burdens. . . . Only by helping the least fortunate of its members to help themselves can the human family achieve the decent, satisfying life that is the right of all people.

Point Four was not to be another giveaway of billions of dollars. The sums voted for "development programs" were comparatively small — only $236 million in 1952, for instance, of which the largest beneficiary country, India, might receive $44 million. The intention was not to provide money so much as advice and technical assistance. It was a case of giving the backward people the "show-how," of helping them to produce, as Truman said, through their own efforts. This meant in the first place missionary work by members of the Technical Co-operation Administration. The T.C.A. could operate only at the invitation of the government of the undeveloped country — invitation which in the case of a few nations, notably Syria, would not be forthcoming — and then must watch carefully that its services were not being used for the political or personal ends of members of that government. It had to be in contact with commercial companies which might be induced to undertake developmental work on a commercial basis. And while working in partnership with the United Nations agencies, it must be ready to step in where those international bodies feared to tread.

Some people thought that rather than set up its own T.C.A. the Americans would have done better to work solely through the United Nations Technical Assistance Administration, F.A.O., WHO, UNESCO and the like, but the United States was already contributing 60 per cent of the money spent by UN agencies on developmental and technical assistance, and were its contribution to be greatly increased, the UN agencies could hardly be felt to be international. If it were not increased, the work could not be done on any big scale except by American initiative, and that meant through Point Four.

Big-scale contributions were not the type of foreign aid which won Americans most affection and respect in the postwar world. More telling from that point of view was the example set by T.C.A. agents in Indian villages or the work done by Americans of the Society of Friends, for example in Lapland, where they went to the assistance of Finns in devastated farmsteads immediately after the war.

THE TREASON SCARE

While the citizens of other democratic countries accepted the policy of Containment as a defensive measure against Russian imperialism, large sections of the American public were inclined to regard it as a crusade against Communism, at home as well as abroad. The American Communist Party had never been strong; its postwar membership was 55,000 and decreasing, and there was not a single acknowledged Communist in electoral public office anywhere in the United States. Nevertheless, the Party was feared as a potential fifth-column, and in 1949 its leaders were charged with violating the Aliens Registration Act (1940) and after a trial drawn out over nine months were convicted and sentenced to fines and imprisonment. Much more disturbing was the thought that there might be traitors in high places. In July 1948 an ex-Communist, Whittaker Chambers, accused certain government officials, including Alger Hiss of the State Department, of having been members of a prewar Communist underground movement. They denied the charges, but Hiss was indicted for perjury in December and his trials dragged on over 1949 and part of 1950. Hiss was found guilty — it appeared that he had been a member of the Communist Party engaged in peddling State documents — and the case left a smear of suspicion over other public servants of hitherto unblemished repute.

Hardly had the Hiss scandal died down when the crusade against Communism was taken up by a new champion of Americanism, Joseph R. McCarthy, a Catholic of Irish descent who sat in the Senate as junior member for Wisconsin. His weapons were the Senate and House investigating committees, admirable constitutional devices for control of the executive by the elected legislature of which McCarthy was able to make abominable misuse. Through these committees he and his coadjutors were able publicly to investigate the loyalty of any civil servant, however unimportant and unrelated to security his position might be, and to extend the witch hunt to state colleges and universities. A congressional committee had the power to subpoena any American citizen or resident and make him testify on oath or face charges of contempt of Congress. As in a court of law, the citizen had the right to refuse to answer questions if he felt that his testimony might lead to self-incrimination; he could fall back on the Fifth Amendment to the Constitution, under which no person is required to testify against himself. But the refusal was taken as the admission of at least some Communist connection and invariably left a smear. McCarthy was an impudent bully whose demagogy at any other time would have had little effect, but when Americans were fighting in Korea and casualty lists were mounting he had the public behind him. Never did he succeed in exposing a single Communist in the State Department or in proving that he had brought to the notice of the Administration any valuable information that it did not already possess, but he was able to arouse a witch hunt all over the United States, in the course of which hundreds of civil servants and teachers were dismissed and thousands felt obliged to resign.

Nothing in the postwar decade did more harm to the good name of the United States than the movement which became known as McCarthyism. It was not the first popular witch hunt in recent American history. In the early 1920's Negro-baiting was a passion in the southern states of the Union and Papist-baiting almost a passion in the north. In the 1930's Father Coughlin won a huge following by preaching anti-Semitism on the radio. By the early 1950's there was no trace of a Popery scare in the United States and racial fears and hatreds were fast diminishing. Perhaps there was one thing to thank McCarthy for: the Communist witch hunt had extinguished all the others.

REPUBLICANS IN OFFICE

The Democrats had been in office for twenty years when the presidential electoral campaign opened in 1952. They seemed to have a good chance of returning their candidate to the White House in the sixth successive election. The man they put forward, Governor Stevenson of Illinois, was certainly a credit to them, but the Republicans nominated General Eisenhower, who, though a soldier of no political experience or acquaintance with domestic affairs, was a popular hero. He won 33 million popular votes — more than any presidential candidate had ever received before — to Stevenson's 26 million, and the long reign of the Democrats was over.

The change made little difference to American external policy. The type of isolation which Right-wing Republicans were advocating in the Senate and the House found no favor with President Eisenhower and Secretary of State Dulles, who had been closely associated with the policy of Truman and Acheson. Containment had begun as a bipartisan policy, and as a bipartisan policy it continued. There were alarums — for instance when Dulles seemed to be supporting Chiang Kai-shek to the extent of possible war against Communist China — but there were no excursions: the Republican administration was always more moderate in practice than in precept. The policy of foreign aid went on much as it had under Truman. Each year after the end of the Korean War the total spending authority asked from Congress was reduced, but in the fiscal year 1955 the Administration was planning to spend about $5 billion in foreign aid. Each year the emphasis shifted a little farther from military and economic aid for Europe to aid for the rest of the world. In view of the economic recovery of Europe and the needs of the United States — particularly its strategic needs — this was right and proper. What the United States needed to import was rubber and tin, chrome, manganese, cobalt and tungsten, none of which commodities could be obtained from Europe. For rubber and tin the Americans had to look to Malaya, Indonesia and Bolivia, the chrome came from Turkey, Southern Rhodesia and South Africa, the manganese from India,

South Africa and the Gold Coast, the cobalt from the Belgian Congo, the tungsten from Bolivia and Siam.

Prosperity continued to rise after the Republicans' accession. There was a slight recession in the latter part of 1953 and the early part of 1954, mainly the result of a decline in government outlays, but the President was able to point out that "although industrial production in the first six months of this year [1954] was running 8 per cent below the level for the first months of 1953 . . . the gross national product showed much smaller decline." By 1955 the economy was running at a rate which compared favorably with 1952, though rather below the record year 1953. Between 1939 and 1953 the total real national product in the United States had approximately doubled. As a Washington journalist remarked, "the period was short enough for the change to be appreciated."

The postwar decade, it has often been said, was an American age, and it is true that no other nation influenced the world so widely and in so many ways. Influence on the military plane was the most obvious: the policy of Containment had established U.S. arms all round the Communist bloc: U.S. bases in Japan and Okinawa, U.S. missions in Formosa and Southern Vietnam, U.S. armaments in Pakistan, Turkey and Greece, U.S. bases again in Morocco, France, Germany and Britain. The United States had led the world, for better or for worse, in the development of nuclear weapons. Economic influence was hardly less obvious than the military and much more important. The hopes and fears of foreigners were fixed on the American economic barometer, the Communists hoping for a slump as profoundly as the non-Communists feared one. Yet it was not so much American trade or even American aid that was so influential: what was influencing the world materially and socially were the distinctively American methods of production. The methods which every country was imitating or hoping to be able to imitate were the American technique of mechanization and mass production and the American ways of concentrating industrial administration and of organizing scientifically the use of labor. "The originality of the American experiment," wrote André Siegfried, "resides essentially in its development of organization. . . . The U.S.S.R. is a disciple, technically speaking, of the United States, and it is on the American plan that the world of today will find its renaissance."

It may be objected that in comparison with its material influence the spiritual influence of the United States was meager. The world which looked up to America for its power, wealth and methods of production was not impressed by American ideology or even by the American way of life. In 1955 American influence was still superficial. But looking back over the ten years, the conclusion must be that it was singularly benign. No other preponderant Power had acted so moderately in its newly realized might, had forced its rule or its ideas on so few foreign people, or had been so enlightened in pursuing its self-interest.

INDEX